DESIGN QUALITY
IN NEW HOUSING

DESIGN QUALITY IN NEW HOUSING

Learning from the Netherlands

MATTHEW COUSINS

Taylor & Francis
Taylor & Francis Group

Frontispiece:
A view from above of new housing at Ypenburg, close to the Hague.

First published 2009
by Taylor & Francis
2 Park Square, Milton Park, Abingdon, Oxon OX14 4RN

Simultaneously published in the USA and Canada
by Taylor & Francis Inc
270 Madison Avenue, New York, NY 10016, USA

Taylor & Francis is an imprint of the Taylor & Francis Group, an informa
business

© 2009 Matthew Cousins

Designed and typeset in Univers by Alex Lazarou, Surbiton
Printed and bound in India by Replika Press Pvt. Ltd, Sonepat, Haryana

British Library Cataloguing in Publication Data
A catalogue record for this book is available from the British Library

Library of Congress Cataloging-in-Publication Data
A catalog record for this book has been requested

ISBN10: 0-415-44769-0 (hbk)
ISBN10: 0-415-44770-4 (pbk)

ISBN13: 978-0-415-44769-0 (hbk)
ISBN13: 978-0-415-44770-6 (pbk)

It is hard to find anyone in the housing development process
who will say that design quality is not important to them ... yet,
new housing remains decidedly uninspiring.
Why?

Commission for Architecture and the Built Environment, *The Housing Audit, Assessing the Design Quality of New Homes, in the East Midlands, the West Midlands and the South West*, London: CABE Publications, 2006, p. 56.

Acknowledgements

Many thanks to James Bynner and Ike Ijeh for their insightful and intelligent debate on Dutch housing. Thank you to Sebastian Macmillian, Tim Crocker, Barbara Weiss, Caroline Mallinder, Ben, Will and Edward Cousins, and Trudy de Mooy at the Information Centre in Vathorst, Amersfoort. Most of all, thanks to Katinka and Julian Cousins for their patience. This book is inspired by and dedicated to my mother Christine Cousins.

Contents

Introduction

Design quality is essential to a better standard of living and is increasingly being accepted as vital to *successful* new housing developments. Good design quality provides robust, attractive and sensitively planned homes that shape communities and helps create a healthier and more advanced society. Yet, design quality is a vague and subjective term and raises many questions – whose judgement of good quality design should be followed, and what values and aspirations of design quality do architects, design and planning professionals need to address to ensure better housing developments?

The British and Dutch governments increasingly refer to design quality when discussing their ambitious proposals for new housing. There are plans for three million new homes to be constructed in the United Kingdom by 2020, and two million new homes in the Netherlands. However, many new homes in the United Kingdom are not being built to the British government's ambitious design standards. The Royal Institute of British Architects considers the quality of UK housing today to be 'extremely disappointing'.[1] The report *The Housing Audit*,

Assessing the Design Quality of New Homes, carried out by the Commission for Architecture and the Built Environment (CABE), found 80 per cent of new housing in the United Kingdom is failing to reach a 'good' or 'very good' standard.[2] The later Housing Audit for the North East, North West, Yorkshire and Humber, published in 2005, also conducted by CABE, assessed only 3 schemes out of 93 as being 'very good' or 'good', the rest being 'average' or 'poor'.[3] In the Netherlands, however, design quality standards have had a more positive evaluation; the Netherlands Ministry of Housing, Spatial Planning and the Environment assessed 92 per cent of new housing as 'good' to 'very good', and only 2 per cent was rated as poor quality.[4]

The poor quality of new housing was further evidenced by Linda Clarke and Christine Wall in 1996.[5] The table beow illustrates that housing developments in the Netherlands have a better quality assessment rating than in the United Kingdom in almost all of the given factors. Clarke and Wall also conclude that Dutch construction projects are built faster than their UK equivalents, and build costs are lower.

There are many complex reasons why new housing in the United Kingdom has been reported to be of poor quality. Michael Ball in *A Troubled Relationship* asserts that the poor quality of the housing industry is derived from the extreme market volatility and a supply system that makes little investment in training within the United Kingdom.[6] The designer Wayne Hemingway believes the problem of low quality is not necessarily a lack of desire on behalf of housebuilders and architects, but an amalgamation of a few sensitive factors such as the planning process, profit margins and confidence.[7] Edwin Heathcote, on the other hand, believes the problem of poor design quality is one of low ambition.[8]

Many architects and built environment professionals have observed that the UK should look to the Netherlands to learn lessons on good quality housing. Researching for his book *A New London*, Richard Rogers travelled to the Netherlands and was inspired by good quality Dutch housing:

> When Mark Fisher and I visited the Netherlands, we discovered that in some cities as much as half of new housing is publicly funded and ... is generally of the highest

Quality assessment in new build houses
in the United Kingdom and the Netherlands

	United Kingdom	Netherlands
Space standards	Low	High
Storage	Low	Medium
Floor finish	Medium	Low
Kitchen finish	High	High
Energy efficiency	Low	High
Environmental specifications	Low	High

Source: Adapted from Linda Clarke and Christine Wall, *Skills and the Construction Process: A Comparative Study of the Vocational Training and Quality in Social Housebuilding*, Bristol, The Policy Press, 1996, p79.

standard. Designed by the Netherlands' bright-est architects, this new local authority housing avoids the mistakes of ... early planning and tends to be highly sensitive to urban context, yet incorporates the spirit of innovation.[9]

In 1998, Richard Rogers and the Urban Task Force cited the quality of housing in the Netherlands as a common reference in *Towards an Urban Renaissance.*[10] The Urban Task Force was impressed by the 'significantly more advanced' standard of housing in the Netherlands, stating that the UK needs to 're-establish the quality of urban design and architecture as in the Netherlands.'[11] Examples of new housing in the Netherlands were later cited in Richard Rogers' and the Greater London Authority report *Housing for a Compact City.*[12]

Dutch methods of design and construction, including those referred to as 'modern methods of construction',[13] are also often mentioned in the British architectural press as represent-ing good quality design. Ricky Burdett, the former adviser on architecture and urbanism to the Mayor of London, believes the design vision for the Thames Gateway in the south-east of England should be sought from the Netherlands, saying, 'We should look at how completed sites similar to the Thames Gateway, such as some in the Netherlands, could be applied to the conditions in London.'[14] Wayne Hemingway, chairman of Building for Life and designer of the Staiths, in Gateshead, believes designers and architects in the UK should learn from good housing such as in Borneo-Sporenburg in the Netherlands:

A model is Amsterdam and the developments on Java, Borneo-Sporenberg islands where progressive urban planners insist on great housing being made available to city residents of poorer areas at sensible prices, allowing

↖ Abbotts Wharf at the Limehouse Cut, East London.

↑ The Abode, Newhall, Harlow.

people normally excluded from the housing market to get on the ladder.[15]

This book attempts to evaluate current thinking about design quality in the Netherlands and the UK. It assesses how architects, planners and built environment professionals can learn lessons from housing in the Netherlands and the United Kingdom to design and deliver better-quality homes. It concludes by recommending new methods of implementing design quality.

What is design quality?

The term design quality is often used in relation to the built environment for ensuring value and competitiveness within the construction industry. It is, however, an ambiguous term and difficult to define. Design quality comprises a number of inter-connected factors based on the aspirations and needs of housing residents and those people involved in the designing of new housing. This consists of the broad characteristics that make up new housing developments, such as site context, location, aesthetical considerations, internal and external features, briefing requirements and constraints.

Design quality is difficult to define because contrasting interpretations are made by the determining parties, such as the house occupier, design team, client and government. A first-time buyer rates price, location and the size of rooms higher than that of build quality and external appearance.[16] Housebuilders, on

← New Dutch housing at Vathorst, Amersfoort.

↓ A housing development on the Thames Gateway
situated close to overhead pylons.

the other hand, are said to determine buildability with stand-ardisation, speed and cost, and good market research before-hand as the most important elements of design quality.[17] The Housing Corporation see design quality as the delivery of desir-able, affordable homes utilising innovative approaches to sat-isfy the needs and aspirations of occupiers.[18] The Home Builders Federation, however, distinguish between product quality, design quality and customer service quality, arguing that design quality falls into two areas, urban design and aesthetic quali-ty.[19] Matthew Carmona, head of planning at University College London, believes that design quality derives from a complex framework of 17 principles that draw on the evolution of hous-ing design, including legibility, homeliness and choice.[20]

It is about tailoring housing to changing needs and about ensuring that dwellings retain their utility value as society changes. Dwellings must provide a high quality of accom-modation over the long term ... Quality is about creating appealing residential environments where people will want to live.[21]

The differing aspirations that parties place on design quality can be seen in the approaches taken by the Dutch and British gov-ernments. Design quality in Dutch housing has been driven by past government statutory measures such as the 1901 Housing Act. More recently, since the early 1990s the Dutch government has emphasised the importance of good quality housing in the Netherlands in a number of key policy documents including a government-sponsored architectural policy. Design quality has also been pursued via the individual, by suppliers of housing and housing services, housing associations and by government authorities.

The Fifth National Policy Document on Spatial Planning, pub-lished in 2001, defined design quality through seven criteria: (1) spatial diversity; (2) economic and social functionalities; (3) cultural diversity; (4) social equality; (5) sustainability; (6) attractiveness; and (7) human scale.[22] These broad headings each cover a range of aspects for good housing design in the Netherlands. *Spatial diversity* refers to the physical composition of a housing scheme including space standards, performance of building regulations, dimensions of buildings, variation of dwelling types, forms and

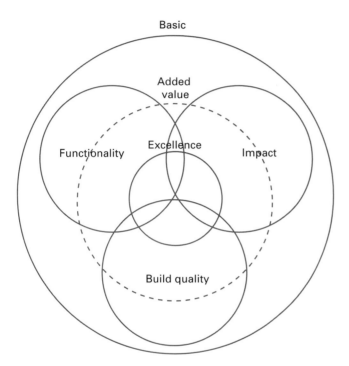

In the United Kingdom design quality has been promoted via a range of mechanisms to control and guide the delivery of new housing, including a number of important policies and design guides. In addition, the government 'encourages' design quality through sponsoring events, awards for housing, funding for schemes and the support of the Commission for Architecture and the Built Environment (CABE). CABE was established in 1999 to promote and encourage high standards in the design of buildings. It has addressed design quality in a number of publications, including: *Urban Design Compendium; Design Review: How CABE Evaluates Quality in Architecture and Urban Design; Housing Audit;* and *By Design, Better Places to Live.*[23]

The *Design Review* affirms that design quality should 'remain as sound a basis for judging architecture now as when [it was] conceived' with the Vitruvian notions of commodity, firmness and delight.[24] In the first century BC Marcus Vitruvius, a Roman architect and engineer, wrote *De Architectura*, known today as *Ten Books On Architecture*. He believed that a building must exhibit the three qualities of *firmitas* (build quality), *utilitas* (functionality) and *venustas* (impact). *Design Review* asserts that all three factors need to be combined when designing and evaluating all aspects of the building process, particularly in new housing, as the 'criteria are intertwined within the design process'.[25] For some architects, the Vitruvian categorisation of design quality still represent an important tool in the process of achieving good quality housing. Sunand Prasad believes that the interconnecting factors of *functionality*, *impact* and *build quality* must be inherent in the design to achieve good design quality (see figure above).[26] Prasad believes the combination of these factors deliver 'added value' to achieve excellence and at the same time raise the average standard of housing.

The CABE *Housing Audit* suggests, however, that there is a pragmatic approach to good design quality in new housing, which can be promoted through four principal aspects, namely (1) character; (2) roads, parking, pedestrianisation; (3) design and construction; and (4) environment and community. These four factors have been further developed into 20 associated factors by the government-supported Building for Life Standard and endorsed by the Home Builders Federation, the Housing Corporation, English Partnerships, the Civic Trust and Design for Homes. It is further stated by CABE and the Building for Life Programme that the successful implementation of these factors provides the apparatus for the design of good quality new housing.

densities. It also accounts for the differences between the city and the countryside. *Economic and social functionalities* refers to investment in community buildings and infrastructure such as railway stations, schools and playgrounds, and to local facilities such as cafes and shopping centres. *Cultural diversity* refers to a diversity of activities for local communities such as community halls, cultural facilities, street art and public spaces. *Social equality* ensures that the design of the housing development reflects the aspirations of the community, including whether the design has an adequate mix of tenure. *Sustainability* refers to reducing the environmental footprint of a housing development. This includes specifying durable and locally sourced materials, and ensuring the housing development achieves the optimum energy performance rating. *Attractiveness* comprises the contribution of the aesthetical characteristics of a housing scheme and the composition of individual dwellings to the overall appearance of the development. *Human scale* includes the urban design of a housing development such as car parking, coherence of street design and easy access to transport. The Dutch case studies in this book have accordingly been assessed against these factors (pages 25–67).

The above-mentioned 20 factors are to cover a broad range of essential design characteristics of a housing development and relate to the four factors as follows. *Character* refers to the identity and composition of a scheme, taking into account topography and landscape, wayfinding, layout and distinctive architectural quality. *Roads, parking and pedestrianisation* refers to the often-overlooked provision of wide and safe streets, public spaces, pedestrian routes and adequate cycle lanes. *Design and construction* includes well-considered internal and external spaces with good proportions. This category also ensures that new housing is suitable for the occupier and conforms to building regulations. *Environment and community* refers to easy access to public transport, appropriate local infrastructure, the planning of community facilities and services. The case studies in this book from the United Kingdom have accordingly been assessed under these four design quality headings (pages 97–127).

Chapters 1 and 2 in this book will assess design quality in both the Netherlands and the United Kingdom with the respective evaluation tools as promoted by each government. Evaluations of design quality in the Netherlands will, therefore, be divided into the seven characteristics from the Fifth National Policy Document on Spatial Planning. Evaluations of design quality in the United Kingdom will be divided into the four characteristics of the CABE Housing Audit.

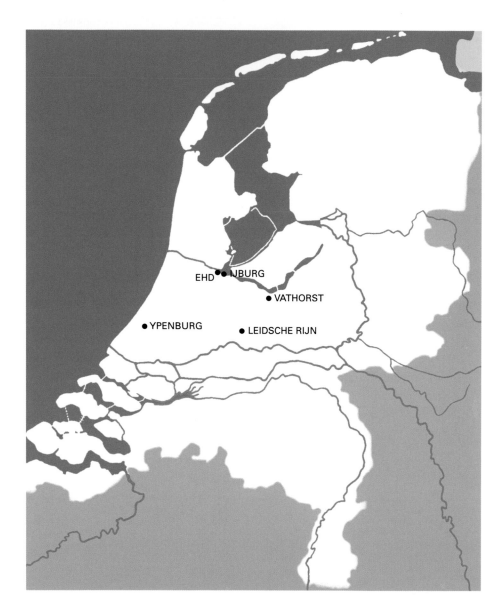

chapter one

Design quality in the Netherlands

Context

The Netherlands boasts a large number of very high-quality new housing developments and has a history of well-designed and distinctive housing. The Dutch government has played a major role in the delivery of new housing and has made design quality an important part of government policy. This can be seen in the role of the government, which is anchored in the constitutional provision to promote and guarantee sufficient availability and quality of housing for its citizens; 'the promotion of sufficient residential accommodation is a subject of concern to the government.'[1] Although the Netherlands is often commended for its innovative and contemporary housing, many new houses in the Netherlands are not built to the highest quality standards. Jonathan Woodroffe, an architect working in the Netherlands, argues:

> Only one per cent of what is being built here is avant-garde. There's a huge amount which is pretty ordinary… It's difficult to build really high quality here.[2]

Furthermore, not everyone in the Netherlands is of the opinion that Dutch housing demonstrates characteristics of good design quality. Many Vinex housing projects have caused controversy and been heavily criticised for their lack of services, poor design and unsustainability:

> The fundamental aims of the Vinex operation are not achieved. The built fabric is not compact. The range of housing options is unbalanced. The amount of differentiation in the programme is negligible. The problem of personal transport is simply aggravated by the total car-dependence. Sustainability loses out, with minimal house dimensions and no scenarios for the future development of these dormitory suburbs.[3]

Due to a rising population and the demand for smaller and more spacious dwellings there is a housing shortage in the Netherlands. It is estimated that between 2010 and 2020 an additional 800,000 new dwellings will have to be built to meet demand.[4] To address this housing shortage the Dutch have taken an innovative and pragmatic approach to the design and planning of new housing. As this book demonstrates, many new houses in the Netherlands have been constructed on large brownfield sites. These include the former military airport at Ypenburg, the former docks at the Eastern Harbour District, or on reclaimed land such as the artificial islands of Ijburg. Other new housing developments have been constructed on green-field sites on farmland outside existing towns such as Vathorst and Leidsche Rijn.

Consensus culture

It has often been commented that the successful design quality of housing in the Netherlands is a result of a consensus culture. Hans Ibelings, in *The Artificial Landscape: Contemporary Architecture, Urbanism, and Landscape Architecture in the Netherlands* asserts that Dutch consensus has led to the protection of the citizen by the government and this in turn has led to good housing:

> The task of the public administration is to provide direction in order to protect weak interests and safeguard collective values.[5]

Historically, there has been a strong culture of collaboration in Dutch politics known as the 'polder-model'. This expression derives from the word polder, or reclaimed land, which describes the historical cultivation of the land from the sea. The concept of the 'polder-model' is one of consensus where all citizens can contribute to their environment. The Netherlands consists of twelve municipalities each with local responsibilities for areas such as the environment, spatial planning and traffic. After acquiring the land for a housing development, the municipality takes responsibility for site preparation, infrastructure and street layout. Municipalities are responsible for drawing up urban development plans of the design of new housing and choosing and appointing design teams. Municipalities also set the requirement of 70 per cent private housing and 30 per cent social housing.

The 'polder model' endorses an integrated framework, which embraces architecture, urban design and landscape design in reclaiming land, planning new housing developments and preserving the *Green Heart* of the Ranstad area from increasing urbanisation. Partnership models in the Netherlands between the municipality, the community and the developer have been established to provide a separation of roles to avoid confusion and conflicts of interest. There is a *projectbureau,* a small multidisciplinary project team, in every town that is responsible for the coordination of major housing projects. Voluntary panels of experts are established jointly by local authorities and development companies and operate as a quality control team judging the quality of design on new housing developments. The government provides indirect support for housing corporations and works with local authorities and private owners to promote good quality housing through the government's architecture policy.

←   Innovative Dutch housing overlooking a canal in Almere.

← New Dutch housing on the reclaimed artificial islands
of Ijburg outside Amsterdam.

→ Experimental housing by Marlies Rohmer Architects
from the exhibition 'Het Wilde Wonen' ('wild housing')
in Almere challenged the architect and client to come
up with new, experimental solutions for building
customised housing.

The concept of an integrated framework is also seen in a regulated planning process in which the public often plays a role in the development and quality of the built environment. The citizen has a voice and can make a direct contribution to the quality of their environment. For example, in 1985, the Spatial Planning Act on the openness of public in administration (*Wet openbaarheid van bestuur*) contained rules about how citizens involved in a planning application in new developments in their local area could make their opinion heard about a key decision that a public body intended to make.

Vuijste and Hooker suggest that the reason for collaboration developed in the 1960s within a liberal government and free-thinking organisational structure of public management.[6] As innovative ideas and influences were imported into the Netherlands in the 1960s, Dutch culture opened up to new possibilities for experimentation. This led to the development of a highly politicised public. In turn, this led to public protests opposing large construction projects such as the city hall and opera house developments in Amsterdam. The Dutch government, further exasperated by criticism of recently completed housing projects, began to re-address its urban and architectural policy.

They fought back because the public cared that their cities were being disfigured and because the discussion about the qualities of urban space was picked up by critics and their readers. Making a collective space has always been a central part of what the Dutch did.[7]

The principle of consensus culture as a way of safeguarding the interests of the government is today widely criticised in the Netherlands. Collaboration also often means that projects take a long time to develop whilst waiting for decisions about government subsidies and public consultation. Peter Boelhouwer, professor of housing at Delft University, argues that developers face particular problems in gaining planning approval due to the length of time municipal authorities take to reach decisions, the lengthy negotiations with local councils, the inadequate skills of council staff and procedures associated with local plans.[8] In many cases this has led to political disputes in the chain of administration as the local council has faced confrontation with government departments. The consensus system is proving unpopular, and its future is widely debated in the Dutch media:

This polder model also accommodates radical proposals, although in practice they are often smothered in compromise, just as nearly everything here gets smothered in compromise. The Dutch could be said to have an over-developed craving for consensus which means not only that the proposals of architects, urban planners, and landscape architects are usually less spectacular in execution than in conception, but also that their implementation is often dogged by lengthy delays. What is lacking in the Dutch culture of consultation and negotiation is decisiveness and promptness of action.[9]

Consensus culture, therefore, has been a driver of good quality design in housing but it has also experienced many political and economic problems. In theory, the consensus culture concept is an attractive model, which aims to give an equal voice to

everyone through the political system. In reality, collaboration is idealistic, as economic forces shape people's values and judgements in everyday life. The quality of housing in the Netherlands has, however, benefited from a consensus culture and this has led to the creation of excellent standards and quality control. As the new housing developments in this book demonstrate, a consensus culture has led to open attitudes towards design quality and the successful creation of new housing.

SuperDutch

Dutch housing projects have received international critical acclaim and have witnessed widely documented architectural publicity. One of the best-known books on contemporary Dutch housing is by Bart Lootsma, who classified well-designed housing as 'SuperDutch'.[10] Lootsma profiles twelve 'radical' design firms including the architectural practices of OMA, MVRDV and Neutelings Riedjijk, and presents the best of the Dutch innovative design projects of the 1990s. In *The Artificial Landscape* Hans Ibelings analyses the contemporary Dutch architecture scene, arguing that the Dutch landscape is artificial, and as a consequence transformable, which has provided a new freedom for architects and designers to design more innovative and self-confident housing. [11]

Many Dutch architecture practices have successfully combined theory with construction projects. Rem Koolhaas and his firm OMA have been at the forefront of Dutch architecture since the early 1980s, when the firm established itself with a number of ground-breaking international competition entries

experimenting with new architectural concepts. The office provided influential training for many young architects who then set up their own offices and developed their own innovative approaches to housing design. Alejandro Zaero-Polo, of the architectural practice Foreign Office Architects, was inspired by the Dutch approach to architecture when he was working as an employee of OMA in the Netherlands and attributes the success of its buildings to management and an understanding of government authorities:

> This high-level management has devised a system in which cultural production and speculation have become perfectly integrated in the making of the environment, and this arrangement is paying handsome dividends... But it is an incredible achievement that such a smooth marriage of theory and practice has been created not by historical coincidence – as in Spain in the '80s – but by artificial arrangement and ruthless determination of competent authorities. [12]

Lootsma and Ibelings also both attribute the raised profile of Dutch architecture and quality of housing to a strong culture of state patronage, an investment in architecture and an architectural policy over the last 15 years. This has developed through a number of government-promoted events and architectural centres. These include the International Biennale Rotterdam (a biennial architectural event exhibiting work in the disciplines of architecture, urban design and landscape architecture), and the Amsterdam Centre for Architecture (ARCAM), founded in 1986, which led to the establishment of other Dutch architectural

←← Colourful housing for the 2001 Housing Expo in Almere.

← Dutch housing by Geurst and Schulze Architects at Leidsche Rijn, Utrecht.

centres throughout the country. In addition, the Netherlands Architectural Institute (NAI) was constructed in Rotterdam in 1993 as a cultural centre and a venue to host architectural exhibitions. An estimated 100,000 people visit the Netherlands Architecture Institute every year.

Other support programmes include Europan, an international competition set up for young architects, Archiprix, an annual award for final year students and the Prix de Rome. Young architects can also apply to the government for start-up loans. The *Architecture in the Netherlands Yearbook* also plays an important informative role in educating professionals and clients about developments in Dutch housing. The yearbook selects around 300 entries and the editors choose 60 projects to visit, with 36 projects documented in detail.

There are also government grants awarded for architecture publications, exhibitions and architectural centres such as the Architecture Fund, the Berlage Institute and Architectuur Lokaal. Architectuur Lokaal was founded from the government's first architectural policy as an independent national information centre for individual citizens, private companies and local authorities. The foundation aims to promote the quality of the built environment. Local communities are encouraged by the national architectural policy to express the idea that architecture is a cultural activity. The local architecture centres act as a platform for the local communities and involved parties to share experiences and information. These centres organise excursions, exhibitions and publications throughout the Netherlands.

Policy for architectural quality

Government policy in the Netherlands has been a key factor in influencing new housing. Design quality in housing has been driven by the Dutch government through the national spatial and architectural policies. This can be illustrated in the main overall objective of the Ministry of Housing, Spatial Planning and Environmental Management, which states it is 'working for a permanent quality of the living environment'.[13]

A number of major events have affected the development of quality housing in the Netherlands. The twentieth century was dominated by the influence of the 1901 Housing Act. This Act legislated for the right for all Dutch citizens to decent-quality housing. It introduced important instruments for intervening in the procurement of social housing and also introduced new building regulations to improve and monitor the quality of housing construction and space standards.[14] The 1901 Housing Act also gave city authorities the power to oversee the aesthetic aspects of housing construction. The Act influenced the design and construction of new housing and urban planning. The most well-known expansion plan was H.P. Berlage for Amsterdam South, where large housing blocks were constructed with uniform height, colour and materials.

After World War II the Dutch government focused on a large-scale housing construction programme that delivered a significant number of rapidly produced houses. A policy was established for the construction of large-scale housing projects within urban areas and some new districts on the outskirts of the existing cities. Many of these rapidly constructed houses were later criticised for their uniformity and poor build quality. As a

← The entrance to Scherf 13 in Leidsche Rijn by SeARCH Architects. Car parking is located underneath the building.

↘ New housing in Ypenburg near The Hague.

↓ Studies of housing blocks in Ijburg by Geurst and Schulze Architects.

result, the Dutch government published the First and Second National Spatial Policy documents, focusing on the modernisation of the Netherlands by satisfying demand and improving the quality of the environment.[15]

In the 1980s, concerned about mass criticism of city renovation and new housing projects, government officials and councillors invited foreign architects and experts to key conferences to debate ideas. A series of high-profile conferences, known as the AIR conferences (Architecture International of Rotterdam), were held to which well-known architects were invited. These conferences encouraged government interest in design and design quality and as a result the government established a state budget allocated to exhibitions, research grants and bursaries. It has been suggested that this resulted in a young, active generation of architects collaborating with government members, civil servants, architectural historians and journalists.

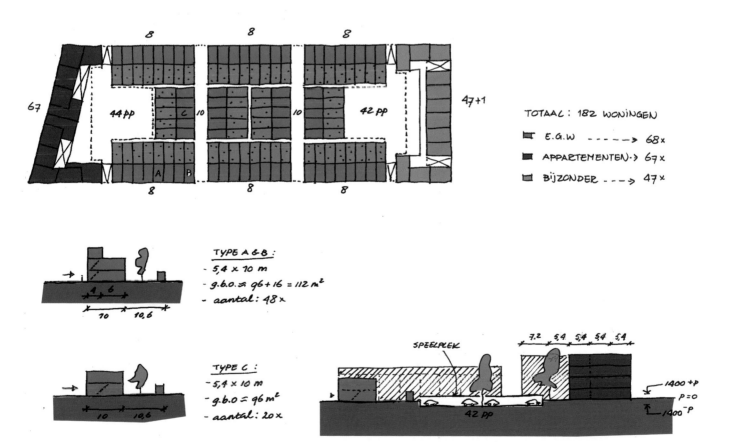

An architectural policy was indirectly born from this debate and a discussion about design quality flourished as a result:

> The message was everywhere the same: the more you talk about architecture, the more it prospers. The halls were full to overflowing. Where previously only architects and the odd critic had shown their face, now there were also aldermen, public servants, housing associations, builders and even one or two property developers.[16]

The Netherlands was the first country in the world to produce a national architecture policy. *Space for Architecture* was published in 1991 by the Ministry of Health, Welfare and Cultural Affairs in collaboration with the Ministry of Housing, Spatial Planning and the Environment. The policy led to the establishment of a number of funds given to the Berlage Institute, the Netherlands Architecture Fund, and Architectuur Lokaal. It also provided the basis for the Netherlands Architecture Institute in Rotterdam. This policy brought together culture and building policy, and aimed to improve architecture and urban design. The main concept in *Space for Architecture* was ensuring architectural quality through three key elements – practical value, cultural value and future value. *Space for Architecture* deliberately avoided making aesthetic judgements on architecture and instead sought to highlight good design practice through demonstrating good design quality in built projects.[17]

The second architectural policy document, *The Architecture of Space*, was published five years later in 1996, broadening the scope of the first policy to include landscape architecture, urban planning and infrastructure. This report sought to highlight good design practice through demonstrating good design quality in built projects.[18]

In 2000, the third architectural policy document was published, entitled *Designing in the Netherlands.* The Dutch Government wanted to meet the public demand for higher quality standards and shape urban renewal and as a result this document included 10 exemplary projects to encourage architectural quality in all sectors of building and urban planning.[19]

In December 2000 the government published the Fifth Policy Document on Spatial Planning, *Making Space, Sharing Space.*[20] It provided guidance on housing development in the Netherlands and contained new policy requirements until 2020. The plans were based on the proposition that the Dutch population will grow to approximately 18 million inhabitants, which would require the construction of up to two million new homes by 2030. To tackle these ambitious proposals the Dutch government proposed that 50 per cent of new homes would be built in existing urban areas on brownfield land, to make more extensive use of the available space and to prevent urban sprawl into the countryside. The Dutch government also highlighted the need for good design quality for the construction of these new homes both at a regional scale and for the private citizen:

> Quality is now defined not only at the higher scale of the main spatial structure, but also at the level of the individual citizen. The space must not [be] allowed to become more monotonous in order to provide citizens with an environment in which to live that meets their wishes and requirements.[21]

→   New Vinex housing in Leidsche Rijn, Utrecht.

↘   New Vinex housing at De Laak in Vathorst, Amersfoort.

The government stipulated that a third of all new homes should be individually commissioned. Individual commissioning is a government-supported programme to allow individuals to acquire the quality of home they desire. Under this programme one or more private individuals acquire land for themselves and commission architects and design professionals of their choice for the design and construction of their homes. The house buyer can choose from a range of variations, use of materials, size and construction methods.

The government will enact new legislation under the 2008 Land Development Act to offer local authorities more opportunities to allocate spare land to individuals under a land policy on the condition that developers adhere to those strict agreements. This is currently a controversial subject in the Netherlands, as due to the size of the country land is scarce and it is not known whether this policy will actually lead to better-quality housing. It does, however, give individuals more choice and freedom to create their own houses, and it creates new styles, forms and construction techniques.

Design quality in Vinex housing

Vinex is an abbreviation of the Dutch term 'Vierde Nota Extra' and was the supplement document to the Fourth National Policy in 1990. The Vinex policy sought to address the balancing of land and space with housing through the long-term goals of durability and high-density housing. This important policy document proposed major changes in Dutch policy to reduce the housing shortage, strengthen the existing transport network and promote high-quality housing projects with higher standards. The housing proposals were ambitious; over a ten-year period from 1995 to 2005 one million houses were to be constructed, close to existing city centres and with good public transport connections. The government provided four billion Euros for the Vinex housing programme, of which 70–80 per cent was for infrastructure.[22] Most of the infrastructure was to be provided by the time a third of the housing was built. There are over 90 new Vinex housing projects in the Netherlands, of which around 50 new towns were built in the Ranstad area between Utrecht and Amsterdam, increasing in total numbers of dwellings by 7 per cent.

Design quality was an important part of the planning of the Vinex housing schemes. Before the towns were designed and

constructed, the Dutch government brought together design panels made up of representatives of the local and regional authorities where the Vinex towns were to be built. These panels were introduced to promote diversity for the proposed designs, to discuss and implement design quality before contracts were signed. Initially, the Vinex concept had strong support from the public due to its associations with the polder-model:

> The new Vinex districts were intended to serve a higher goal than simply the provision of housing. Through a selective choice of development locations, the intention was to contribute to the protection of the open rural areas and to encourage greater use of public transport and the bicycle.[23]

Opinion changed, however, when residents began to see the reality of what was being constructed. There was widespread criticism of the uniform low-rise housing districts. These were said to be the result of contradictory government objectives to implement design quality as described in the architecture policy.[24]

> In short, there is variation aplenty and yet no variation at all. The façade changes, as do the amenities added during the final phase of design, but behind the different elevations lies the same cramped standard dwelling...In effect it ridicules the whole notion of quality envisaged by architectural policy with its assumption of integrity and depth.[25]

One prominent Dutch MP who visited an early Vinex construction site was so disappointed with what he perceived as a 'lack of spatial quality' that he raised the matter in Parliament.[26]

In 1994 a survey of Vinex developments criticised the 'general trend towards mono-functional residential areas with a one-sided housing supply'.[27] A second report, carried out in 1998 for the Netherlands Architecture Fund, went further in its criticism to state there was little trace of the original Vinex objectives. The report's author, Lodewijk Baljon, stated there were three areas of weakness within the constructed housing schemes: the dearth of space for future developments, the poor connection between the new districts and the problematic monotonous character of the new schemes.[28]

> The hope that the Vinex districts would profit from the atmosphere, character and history of an existing city, as envisaged by the Leidsche Rijn masterplan, seems vain. In reality they are more likely to turn out to be autonomous, introverted housing estates whose relation to the city is at most one of proximity. The spatial and social embedding in the existing cities, so crucial to the Vinex idea, is seldom convincing.[29]

Carel Weeber, the former president of The Royal Netherlands Association of Architects, was a strong critic of the Vinex districts. He called them 'state architecture', asserting that their design was used as a means of attracting political and financial support. Weeber called for lower densities and more individual freedom for residents. He suggested the poor quality of these districts had resulted from the consensus culture in the Netherlands, which, he claimed, stifles the fruition of good quality architecture.

> Supervisors, quality teams, plus the real or the imagined lists of names employed by the bigger municipalities in order to promote preferred architects and safeguard

quality. It is striking how much design energy is invested – and wasted – in processes like these...only to be filed away or disappear into some desk drawer. Many designs in the Netherlands are no longer part of the actual production of the built environment, but belong to the world of consultancy and advice, where architecture, urbanism and landscape architecture have been increasingly ending up.[30]

In 2000, there was a re-evaluation of the Vinex policy with the publication of the document *Discussions on Urbanisation to 2010*, which sought to improve the quality of new housing.[31] The document *What People Want, Where People Live* stated in 2001 that the residential environment of Vinex housing was considered inadequate, as the dwellings were:

Too small and without a flexible layout, inadequate parking facilities, a lack of fine-tuning between housing development, infrastructure and mass transit, insufficient amenities and unsuccessful attempt[s] at mixed used development and other much cited drawbacks.[32]

The Vinex housing developments have also been criticised for having a more suburban character than existing Dutch suburbs. Hans Ibelings believes that despite the high density and urban aspirations of the Eastern Harbour District, the peninsulas have acquired a 'suburban character' due to the lack of shops and facilities.[33] Ibelings argues that the Vinex schemes do not resemble the compact city but part of the network city and have become super-Vinex districts, classified as 'Super compact residential developments, super close to the old city centre.'[34] Jaap Evert Abrahamse, however, believes the Vinex model is neither suburban nor part of the city. 'Vinex districts are often depicted as neither fish nor flesh, not metropolitan but not really suburban either'.[35]

The Vinex housing developments, therefore, were established with high ambitions but were later heavily criticised. As the case studies on pages 25–67 demonstrate, however, the new Vinex housing schemes have evolved from the early criticisms and can be seen as examples of successful design quality.

Sustainability

The Netherlands is at the forefront of sustainable housing construction and its national standard for housing is accepted as a benchmark for good sustainable practice. As the case studies in this book illustrate, sustainability is a key component in the design of new housing developments. Throughout the latter half of the twentieth century the Netherlands has sought inventive approaches towards sustainable design, not least because of the concern about the vulnerability of Dutch people to increasing sea levels and the Netherlands' small land mass. In the 1970s the Dutch government explored options of self-sufficiency, striving to improve the environmental efficiency of housing developments. The efficiency of heating and lighting was evaluated and sustainable features such as grass roofs, compost toilets and techniques to improve insulation were explored.[36] In 1974 the Dutch government published its first energy policy document and subsidised the construction of several energy-efficient housing projects. The government was the first in Europe to adopt the principles of the Brundtland Report of 1987, which formed the basis for a number of national energy and planning policies and established the local political agenda on sustainability.

In 1988 the report *Zorgen Voor Morgen* focused on the environmental status of the Netherlands as a whole. The later Environmental Policy Plan, published in 1989, was based on this report.[37] This plan placed more emphasis on energy saving and the reduction in climate change gases. A significant housing project constructed with sustainable ideas from this period was Ecolonia in the municipality of Alphen aan den Rijn. Sustainable design within this housing development incorporated solar boilers, heat buffers, high-efficiency glazing and cellulose insulation and was seen as a model of sustainable living.

Since the early 1990s there have been several government initiatives to stimulate sustainable housing in the Netherlands. In 1993, the policy document of *Environmental Tasks in the Construction Industry* demanded close cooperation in sustainable building practices between the government and the construction industry.[38] In 1996, the Dutch government introduced the National Sustainable Building Packages through the Ministry of Housing, Spatial Planning and Environment and the Ministry for Economic Affairs. This document highlighted the need for higher sustainable standards and focused on implementing sustainable design in the new Vinex projects.[39]

↙   New Dutch housing such as in Ypenburg has been designed to maximise views to the existing lakes, canals and landscape.

→   The diverse streetscape at Vathorst, Amersfoort, combines the design of the traditional Dutch house with the dynamic form and colour of contemporary housing. The fish sculptures represent a theme of water.

In 1995 the Energy Performance Standards were set up by means of a so-called Energy Performance Coefficient for new housing. These standards determined the quantity of energy a building can use. The standards are enforced in the Dutch Building Code, with a target to achieve a 30 per cent efficiency improvement in carbon dioxide emissions by 2020.

The Dutch government requires local authorities to create a demand for green housing via the planning system, with an ability to control unsustainable development. The planning authority has to ensure it enforces a percentage of sustainable housing and set targets for energy use. The government has encouraged new green technology by placing incentives on wind energy and has set a target that all new houses will be built to carbon zero standards by 2020. This target is four years later than the same target set by the British government.

The Dutch Green Financing scheme is an incentive by the Dutch government to stimulate sustainable building as required by the National Guidelines for Sustainable Building. The incentive applies for newly built residential buildings and renovation of housing. Housing developments in the Netherlands that have significantly better environmental performance than required in the building regulations are given a government loan of Green Funding at a lower interest rate than a regular mortgage.

Skills and training

Poor skills in the built environment have been identified as a key barrier to the delivery of good design quality. Linda Clarke found that the Netherlands has a higher quality of housing than in the United Kingdom due to the level of integrated training, skill and productivity of the Dutch construction industry.[40] Clarke suggests that in the Netherlands training is seen as an investment, while it is seen as an extra cost in the United Kingdom. She believes the Dutch construction industry training programme provides a multi-skilled workforce with theoretical and educational grounding where trainees learn different trades, rather than the one trade learned in the United Kingdom. Clarke argues that the United Kingdom needs to build a workforce that is more skilled and qualified in all aspects of construction, with more complex, more multi-skilled interface coordination.

Training in the Netherlands is regulated at the national, regional and local level by committees consisting of representatives of employers, organisations and trade unions. The Dutch construction industry has strong interdependent foundations, with industry training centres that are partly subsidised by the state and partly funded by different companies in the construction industry.

A particular feature of the Dutch construction training system is that it is modular-based. From the outset of the programme students can choose one optional module per year from a different trade. Specialisation is the result of combining the appropriate modules during training. To complete the training programme, trainees must pass 20 modules of continuous assessment with a practical and written examination. Apprentices are taught a broad range of skills and are as a result more flexible and more efficient. Over 80 per cent of apprentice training occurs within the training corporations, where locally based employers run specialist workshops.

The ratio of trainees who are learning trades to construction workers in the Netherlands is double that found in the United Kingdom.[41] The value of the training investment and construction

output per employee is also double in the Netherlands to in the United Kingdom. Linda Clarke argues that constructors use more complex techniques, indicated by the number of subcontractors on site, and there is a higher complexity of interfaces. whereas in the United Kingdom interfaces are more traditional in nature.

In the Dutch case studies on pages 25–67 successful design quality can be attributed to effective training and retention of skills among the participants of the design team, planning department, local and central government departments. For example, for the design of the housing development at Vathorst members of the planning authority, design team and development companies who had worked on the previous development at Kattenbroek were appointed to positions of authority where their experience would help achieve greater quality and consistency for the development at Vathorst. Their experience was therefore retained, contributing to a delivery in quality.

Design quality in the Netherlands

As we have seen, design quality in Dutch housing has been driven by government statutory measures and more recently through a number of key policy documents, including a government-sponsored architectural policy. The Dutch government contends that design quality has been pursued through three separate routes: (1) at individual level everyone must be prepared to assume more responsibility for the quality of both housing and the environment; (2) suppliers of housing and housing services should adopt a far more consumer-orientated attitude and improve the information supply to the public via quality marks and certificates; (3) governmental authorities must ensure that the public is duly involved in the plan development phase.[42]

The government is also pursuing higher standards of quality through the use of Dutch building regulation standards. Technical building regulations are laid down in the Housing Act and a Building Code (named the Building Decree, *Bouwbesluit*) which came into force on 1 January 2003. These are national, uniform and performance-based regulations that designers must comply with for any building. They include a reduction

in the length of time to obtain planning permission, an amendment of the local authority assessment method concerning the appearance of buildings to be more objective, and the standardisation of procedures for applying for a building permit through technical building regulations.

In February 2007 the Dutch government attempted to promote higher quality in construction by setting as a standard a number of minimum requirements in the Building Decree. To improve the restructuring of old urban neighbourhoods, the government has amended the minimum requirements for ceilings (raised from 2.40 metres to 2.60 metres), heights of doors, dimensions of sanitary areas, staircase design, hallway widths and the dimensions of lifts within flats.[43] In the future, decisions about an application for building permission should be made within three months of receipt, with the possibility of extending this for a further three months. The government also intends to change the minimum dimensions of the width of buildings from 5.0 metres to 5.40 metres to increase the flexibility of the dwelling, making it easier to modify the design.

The Dutch government has also introduced quality grades and certificates for housing called *Woonkeurmerken*, which can be obtained voluntarily by buyers, tenants, owner-occupiers and construction firms. These quality certificates relate to the quality of hidden or apparent elements of new or existing dwellings, such as central heating installations, boilers, materials and energy efficiency. The Foundation for Building Quality, the SBK (*Stichting Bouwkwalitet*), an independent foundation under the sponsorship of the Ministry of Housing, Physical Planning and the Environment, manages the most widely used construction quality mark scheme, the KOMO mark, but does not itself carry out the testing inspection or certification, which is instead carried out by a number of independent organisations. The SBK also has a coordinating function on matters relating to quality of construction products, providing a main forum for discussion within the Dutch construction industry on EU quality issues.

Stringent aesthetic requirements, called *Welstandseisen*, must also be met when constructing new extensions and adapting existing features of a dwelling such as roof dormers, bay windows, and colours. These requirements are formulated by special aesthetic committees known as *Welstandcommissies*, appointed by individual councils, and since 2003 municipalities are obliged by the government to adhere to these requirements. If the appearance of an external feature of a dwelling does not comply with the standards set by the commission, a building permit can be refused.

The Eastern Harbour District, Amsterdam

Context

The Eastern Harbour District in Amsterdam is an example of good design quality in new housing and has been highly commended by architects and design professionals. Richard Rogers cites the development as an exemplary housing project in the Greater London Authority document *Housing for a Compact City*.[44] Many local authorities and planning departments have used the district as a model of good new housing, and the designer Wayne Hemingway was inspired by the Eastern Harbour District when designing the Staiths housing in Gateshead:

> We found affordable housing solutions that were visually stimulating and allowed the resident to recognise and describe their house by virtue of its individuality. We found attention to detail in matching downpipe to window frames and coordinated street furniture that was lacking in the UK.[45]

The Eastern Harbour District is situated on the edge of the city of Amsterdam on three connected peninsulas. The district has recently been developed into different neighbourhoods by the City Council of Amsterdam and the local authority, who are keen to maximise the potential for the existing docks area. Each neighbourhood had its own urban planning regulations and controlled development phases took place over 20 years. Each neighbourhood was built over a period of five years, starting in 1985 with the district of Abattoir (1985–1992), followed by Entrepot, KNSM Island (1990–1995), Java Island (1994–2001), Borneo-Sporenburg (1997–2002) and Rietlanden (1998–2003).

The district was formerly a prosperous harbour for the shipment of goods serving the Dutch empire in the Far East. After the economic boom at the end of the nineteenth century the docks gradually declined and in the 1970s became one of the most run-down areas in Amsterdam. Under the motto 'Back to the city' planning policy makers sought to create favourable living conditions. The location of the peninsulas near the centre meant the district was allocated as a key potential area for development. The city council proposed the development of high-density housing on the peninsulas and on the mainland parallel to the islands. Initial policy proposals were to have a density of 100 dwellings per hectare, with a mixture of functions and activities within brownfield land sites in the centre of the city, but without

↑↑ The Eastern Harbour District today.

↑ The Eastern Harbour District as a former harbour for the shipment of goods serving the Dutch empire in the Far East

heavy traffic and industry.[46] New ideas for the district derived from Dutch planning policies on the compact city concept and mixed-use development. The main planning objective was to halt the decrease in the number of inhabitants by increasing the quality and quantity of the housing stock and the level of employment.[47]

The initial designs proposed filling in the water around the docks to create more land for housing developments. The residents, many of whom lived in houseboats and self-made homes, objected to these proposals, stating that the islands should be preserved as they belonged to an important part of the city's

↖ The end apartment block facing the open water on Borneo Island by Dick Van Gameren Architects.

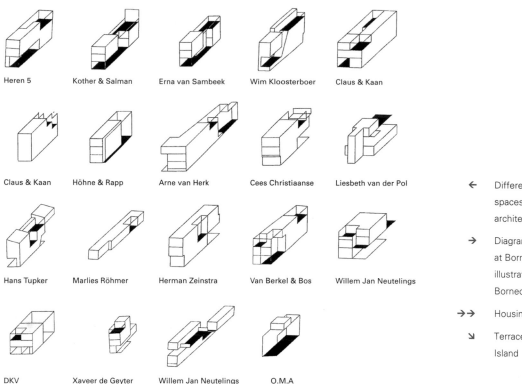

Heren 5   Kother & Salman   Erna van Sambeek   Wim Kloosterboer   Claus & Kaan

Claus & Kaan   Höhne & Rapp   Arne van Herk   Cees Christiaanse   Liesbeth van der Pol

Hans Tupker   Marlies Röhmer   Herman Zeinstra   Van Berkel & Bos   Willem Jan Neutelings

DKV   Xaveer de Geyter   Willem Jan Neutelings   O.M.A

← Different house typologies of solid and void spaces in Borneo-Sporenburg by various architects.

→ Diagram (top) illustrating the internal spaces at Borneo-Sporenburg and diagram (bottom) illustrating the arrangement of blocks at Borneo-Sporenburg.

→→ Housing alongside a canal on Java Island.

↘ Terraced waterside housing on Borneo Island

industrial history. On KNSM Island, hundreds of squatters and houseboat residents objected to the removal of their homes. Squatters challenged the council's intention of infilling the docks and protested against the proposed development with the slogan 'Blue is Green'. In 1988, a referendum was held in favour of the development. However, it was decided to abandon the early plans of filling in the docks and instead to preserve the existing waterfront.

The masterplan for Java Island was designed by the architect Sjoerd Soeters in 1993. Soeters proposed continuous vertical facades of apartment buildings, reflecting the typical traditional houses in the centre of Amsterdam. The canal houses were designed by a number of different young architects who were encouraged to be as creative as possible within certain pre-scribed requirements, such as the width of housing and a deline-ation of public and private spaces. These designs were repeated on different parts of the islands, overlooking the canals that cross the peninsula, creating a collage of dwelling types.

Java Island has been widely praised for its innovative design and planning. In the first years of use, however, the district received mixed reports. Some residents praised its 'extraordi-nary design, its trendy atmosphere, the architecture, the artists and their studios'.[48] Other residents, however, felt that Java Island lacked identity and was designed by 'in-bred architects, resulting in middle class neighbourhoods'.[49] Furthermore, resi-dents thought the structure was too uniform as it consisted of repetitions of identical units. Some felt that the houses were 'too

small and in too high a density, the amenities were substandard, public spaces were scarce, and young persons were extremely bored because there were no recreational facilities.'[50]

Borneo-Sporenburg displays the most innovative and diverse designs out of all islands of the Eastern Harbour District. The brief was set by the city authorities to generate new models of higher density inner-city development at 100 dwellings per hectare, which could accommodate mainly low-rise housing near the city centre. The landscape architecture firm West 8 was selected in an invited competition on the basis of their concept of a 'sea of houses'. The design of the low-rise buildings was characterised by their arrangement of patios and roof terraces, which sought to maximise privacy. West 8 were responsible for a number of elements of the urban plan including the master plan, the design of building typologies, architect supervision, public space, the design of the three bridges and designs for the courtyards. The success of the design led to the develop-ment company New Deal to commission the trial development and construction of 250 dwellings on Borneo-Sporenburg. The project received huge interest and all the trial houses were sold on the basis of their proposed drawings before construction had started.

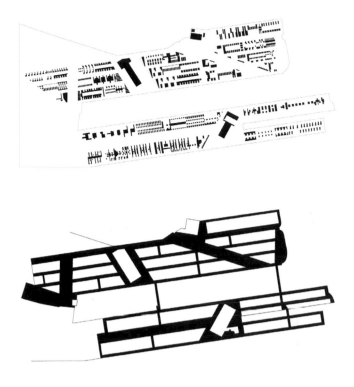

Spatial diversity
and attractiveness

The Eastern Harbour District is made up of a number of peninsulas with a variety of neighbourhoods. The district is unique in containing a variety of experimental low-rise houses, interspersed with attractive higher density housing apartment blocks and canals. It is this diversity and architectural creativity that makes the district a model of good design quality.

Over one hundred architects were involved in designing individual dwellings on Borneo-Sporenburg, resulting in new housing prototypes with roof gardens and good views across the basin. The master plan was based on a new approach to the demands of single family houses, providing generous outdoor space, a secure parking space, safety and individuality. The design was achieved under strict urban planning and architectural guidelines. A design code was established that created consistency and unity among individual designs. There were design codes for streetscape, parking, private open space, height and plot width. The design code also required a 30 per cent to 50 per cent void in each of the individual homes to ensure maximum light would enter the building and to further enhance the diversity of the design. As a result, most dwellings have a 3.5 metre high ground floor, allowing maximum light to penetrate deep into the living room on the upper floor.

The master plan by West 8 landscape architects was based on a simple rectilinear grid of terraced streets. They developed a typology in which a small patio served for daylight penetration and personal outdoor space. On Scheepstimmermanstraat, a double block of 100 dwellings was sold to individual owners, creating many diverse and inventive designs in which 19 different architects designed 56 narrow canal houses. Each building's owner commissioned an architect of their choice and was able to choose a design for the internal and external appearance of their house.

On Java Island, the buildings facing the quays were all restricted to 27 metres wide with the same palette of materials and colours across as the island. A structural grid with a bay size of 5.4 metres was designed along the entire length of both quays, only interrupted by intersecting canals. Each building had its own briefing requirements of function, access and design.

Economic functionalities, cultural diversity and social equality

There is a mixture of tenure across the peninsulas. The district was developed at first by the public sector with public funding, but later was funded by private companies under the control of the local council. The first constructed dwellings consisted of 100 per cent social housing at the Abattoir site. This reduced to 60 per cent of social housing on KNSM Island and 30 per cent of social housing at Borneo-Sporenburg.

The early planning proposals of the Eastern Harbour District sought to attract a certain number of businesses and jobs into the area. In 1987, the initial planning proposal was to create 800

jobs within the district. In 2002, however, the Eastern Harbour District had 1,541 businesses with 4,197 full-time employees and 408 part-time employees. The businesses were mostly made up of small companies with one or two employees, and with most employment in the service sector.[51] Employers and entrepreneurs stated that the quality of the housing was an important reason why they chose to move their business in the Eastern Harbour District. The first most important factor to entrepreneurs was accessibility by car and the location close to the city centre. The second reason was the quality of the built environment and the third reason was the urban structure and architectural design.[52] Some residents, however, were less satisfied; 40 per cent of the interviewees said the density was too high and the parking facilities were insufficient.[53]

The intentional pursuit of mixed land use at a low spatial scale, the urban/ architectural design, an attractive living environment and good accessibility contributed to the success of the area...It seems that an area with a mixture of dimensions, a fine and sharp grain, and a high degree of interweaving has positive impacts on the perception of the area.[54]

←← Different house typologies of solid and void spaces in Borneo-Sporenburg by various architects.

← Housing by Palmboom and Van Den Bout Architects in Borneo-Sporenburg.

The district is close to the centre of Amsterdam – a 15 minutes cycle ride and five minute car journey. There are small public spaces of landscaped courtyards or gardens but no larger parks as the surrounding water acts as the dominant public space. On Java Island there are public squares and parks in the central spine of the island that shield the garden side of the canal houses. There is a school and housing for the elderly on Borneo-Sporenburg.

Human scale and sustainability

The streets in Borneo-Sporenburg have space for a single lane of traffic, a parking lane, a bike lane and footpath. One parking space is allocated to each house, and three different kinds of parking were planned in the district – a car park, on-street parking and a half-sunken garage. Some low-rise terraced houses also have internal carports and some houses overlooking the canals have private waterfront access. There is provision for bicycles in the streets with a number of bicycle racks. On Java Island, car parking is kept to the periphery of the housing apartment blocks next to the water's edge. There is a single internal pedestrian path running through the centre of the landscaped

courtyard to the middle of the island. Three bridges connect the different peninsulas and have become a characteristic feature of the development. There are two bridges across the 93 metre wide basin, one central low bridge for cyclists and a 12 metre high bridge that provides boats with access to the marina. There are two small parks – the main central KNSM Laan Park and a smaller park, the Small Green Company Park. A number of trees have been planted alongside one of the waterways and all along the main central avenues. Some residents believe there is a lack of greenery and landscaping. Residents reportedly try to take over areas in the already-congested streets and claim it for planting. 'Slow-motion green guerrilla warfare has been waged over the years, in which the residents are trying to take over the streets bit by bit.'[55]

The Eastern Harbour District, Amsterdam

General

Site area 50 hectares Borneo: 13.1 hectares Sporenburg: 10.3 hectares	**Density** Average of 100 density per hectare
Total number of inhabitants/dwellings 17,000 dwellings Borneo and Sporenburg have 2,500 dwellings	**Housing mix by tenure** Mixed tenure. It was 100% public sector now 30% public sector
Average number of people per dwelling 2	**Percentage of commercial use** 3%

Spatial diversity

	Objectives	Strengths	Weaknesses	Evaluation	Design quality standard
1.	Does the scheme exploit existing buildings, landscape or topography?	Very good use of the former docks and water basins.	—	Good initial urban design and planning which exploits the site and water.	Very good
2.	Is there a variety in the types and sizes of housing?	Excellent variety in the types and sizes of housing.	—	Good example of housing designed for diversity but restricted under a design code.	Very good
3.	Do buildings or spaces outperform statutory minima, such as building regulations?	—	—	Advances in ceiling heights and areas for some individual houses. Many houses complying with building standards but not outperforming them.	Good

Economic and social functionalities

	Objectives	Strengths	Weaknesses	Evaluation	Design quality standard
4.	Is there a mix of accommodation and community facilities that reflects the needs and aspirations of the local community?	There is a school and housing for the elderly on Borneo-Sporenburg.	Lack of shops, restaurants and retail area.	The site lacks shops and facilities but is only 15 minutes' cycle ride to the centre of Amsterdam.	Good
5.	Is there a range of living, working and leisure facilities?	Good range of living and some working facilities.	Lack of leisure and shopping facilities.	Good mix of housing and facilities.	Good

Cultural Diversity

	Objectives	Strengths	Weaknesses	Evaluation	Design quality standard
6.	Is public space well designed and does it have suitable management arrangements in place?	A number of small infill public spaces and parks.	Not enough green spaces and public spaces but this is due to the constraints of the peninsulas.	The surrounding water acts as the dominant public space.	Good
7.	Are there any technological innovations?	—	—	High levels of architectural experimentation and innovations in new spatial arrangements, materiality and diversity.	Good
8.	Does the housing scheme have any historical and cultural precedents?	The design features a good range of historical and cultural features from Amsterdam's centre.	—	Well-considered design with experimental approach to precedent.	Very good

Social Equality

	Objectives	Strengths	Weaknesses	Evaluation	Design quality standard
9.	Is there a tenure mix that reflects the needs of the local community?	The different districts have implemented individual approachs to the mix of tenure.	Reports of lack of shopping facilities.	Good mix of housing with tall tower blocks, larger housing schemes and individual houses.	Good

Sustainability

	Objectives	Strengths	Weaknesses	Evaluation	Design quality standard
10.	What design features are in place to reduce the environmental impact?	—	Sustainable features have not been as well considered on the islands.	Sustainable features not well considered.	Average
11.	Does the master plan have a coherent sustainable plan?	A number of small parks.	Many individual buildings lack sustainable features.	Good decision to keep the former docks and not to infill the basins.	Average

Attractiveness

	Objectives	Strengths	Weaknesses	Evaluation	Design quality standard
12.	Do buildings exhibit architectural quality?	Good architectural design with excellent quality.	—	Each district manifests the architectural and urban design ideas of the period.	Very good
13.	Has the scheme made use of advances in construction or technology that enhance its performance, quality and attractiveness?	Good experimental advances in construction of individual houses and larger apartment blocks.	—	Good construction and architectural features which enhance quality.	Good
14.	Does the scheme feel like a place with a distinctive character?	Good mixture of housing between islands and with the large blocks of Piraeus, The Whale, creating diversity of different heights.	Some buildings are, however, less successful and do not look in keeping with the character of other buildings.	Excellent design externally and internally with good variety of housing replicating the variety of housing alongside canals in Amsterdam.	Very good

Human scale

	Objectives	Strengths	Weaknesses	Evaluation	Design quality standard
15.	Does the development have easy access to public transport?	Only 15 minutes by bicycle to the city centre of Amsterdam.	—	Good public transport with a number of buses and trams linking the District to the centre.	Very good
16.	Are public spaces and pedestrian routes overlooked and do they feel safe?	The waterways and large housing blocks such as the Piraeus and the Whale give a sense of orientation. Streets are well overlooked making public spaces feel safe.	—	The three bridges give a structured focus for the islands with clear and well planned roads on the islands.	Very good
17.	Does the scheme exploit existing buildings, landscape or topography?	—	—	Very good use of site constraints of island with parks in the centre of Java island and crossing canals. Good planning of bridges and maximisation of opportunities taken.	Very good
18.	Are the streets pedestrian, cycle and vehicle friendly?	Good use of footpaths and cycle lanes and bridges to and from site and local transport is excellent.	It is very easy to fall into the water over the edge of street level as there are no railings.	Cycle lanes and footpaths very well considered although it is very easy to fall into the water.	Good
19.	Are car parking and roads well integrated so they support the street scene and surrounding development?	Car parking is kept to the periphery of the blocks next to the water's edge. Private garages on Borneo very well designed and supporting street scene.	Lack of car parking spaces.	Excellent layout and variety of housing with parks in centre of Java Island and good use of surrounding water. On Java and KNSM street car parking. On Borneo some private car parking and some street parking.	Good
20.	Are streets defined by a coherent and well-planned layout?	Wider roads on edge of water on Java and KNSM. Borneo has smaller roads in centre of island between houses. Very good planning roads, bridges and footpaths.	—	Good integration to the mainland by three bridges.	Good

Ijburg, Amsterdam

Context

Ijburg is an archipelago of seven artificial islands on newly reclaimed land in the inland sea of Ijmeer on the eastern edge of Amsterdam. When completed, this sand-dredged development will consist of 18,000 new dwellings for 45,000 residents with a variety of dwelling types and a high density of 60 dwellings per hectare. Seven thousand houses have already been built; the remainder of the site is still undergoing construction.

The first phase of the development consists of Havebeiland (Harbour Island), Steigereiland (Jetty Island) and Rieteiland (Reed Islands). Rieteiland comprises of three islands – Groot Rieteiland, Kleine Rieteiland and Rieteiland Zuid. Groot Rieteiland is similar to Haveneiland but the streets are narrower and the houses are smaller. Rieteiland Zuid, however, has a different character as all the housing plots are self-build, with individually commissioned and designed houses. The majority of houses contain large gardens and all have associated facilities including tennis courts and a riding school. The second phase of the Ijburg development consists of Centrumeiland (Centre Island), Middeneiland (Middle Island), Strandeiland (Beach Island) and Buiteneiland (Outer Island), which is currently under construction.

The design of new housing on these islands has had a number of interesting influences. The district has been designed as a contemporary version of nineteenth and twentieth century Amsterdam, with enclosed residential rectangular housing blocks, positioned adjacent to a network of canals. The design has used the models of the varied density of mews streets in Marylebone in London and the uniformity of a rectangular grid of the Sunset District of San Francisco as a precedent. A target ratio of living and working of 1:1 was planned to mirror that of Amsterdam's older southern quarter. Good design quality on Ijburg is the result of a combination of factors: a strong urban programme, a quality team that oversees the design and construction of every housing block and individual house, and the implementation of good architects and built environment professionals early in the development process. The briefing programme for the islands was divided into two distinct components. The local authority developed and managed the publicly funded housing whilst private companies constructed private housing.

On Kleine Rieteiland, private self-build plots were commissioned by private individuals working with an architect of their choice without a supervisory architect and without any aesthetic

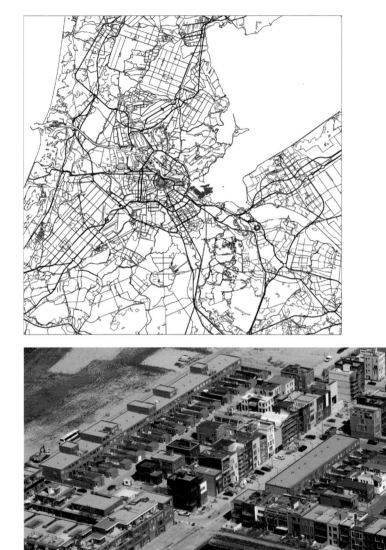

↑↑   A map of the new islands of Ijburg outside Amsterdam.

↑   Steigereiland, Ijburg from above. The seven islands have been designed with maximum diversity in mind with districts comprising of individual terraced houses, a district of large private houses and other districts as social housing with private apartments.

↖   Waterside housing on Haveneiland, Ijburg.

control by the Planning Inspectorate, resulting in a high degree of architectural variation. This freedom has given architects an open invitation to experiment and push the designs to the limit. Architects therefore had to be inventive; they rethought the formal functions of the buildings and designed housing blocks to be deeper and narrower, to let more light enter each apartment. Each block was restricted to accommodate 200 apartments and to contain a mixture of housing and commercial space. Individual self-build plots were planned among the blocks to break up monotony and create diversity. A number of blocks were also left undeveloped for future construction.

In order to ensure design quality, the city council appointed a quality team. Each architect or designer that worked on a housing block on Ijburg was placed under the supervision of a block principal called a 'coach' who supervised an entire design and construction process of an apartment block. The principal also checked the functionality of the block with commercial spaces and the mix of houses and services. The architect and the block principal had to report to a supervising team consisting of the architects Felix Claus, Frits Palmboom, Michael van Gassel, Jaap van den Bout, the urban planner Ton Schaap, the landscape architect Micheal van Gessel, the chairman of the

aesthetic control commission Aart Oxenaar and the chairman of the team Kees Rijnboutt. This group operated as an autonomous quality team that worked in its own independent capacity above the operating parties, enforcing consistency and control. All designs were also analysed by an amenities inspectorate and an expert design panel.

Nobody can simply choose the path of least resistance and trot out a design on autopilot. This way, every architect

←← Colourful terraced housing has been designed by different architects to maximise variety and form.

← An apartment block on Ijburg.

is forced into the role of escapologist, in the often justifiable expectation that the more complicated the situation in which building is to be done, the more ingenious the solutions found to overcome the limitations.[56]

Spatial diversity and attractiveness

The design of Ijburg is visually attractive, with different characteristics for each island. There are many unique, colourful, fresh and innovative high-quality apartments and houses. The urban design is based on a grid of rectangular blocks, rectilinear streets, green strips and waterways. The urban programme for Havebeiland and Rieteiland consists of a grid of large urban blocks with a variety of streets, avenues, canals, squares and quays, all modelled on characteristics of the historical city of Amsterdam. These districts were planned so that each grid within the master plan would have a number of apartment blocks and each block would have its own programme of housing, business and communal facilities containing a wide mix of dwelling types, offices, local services and general amenities. Each apartment block was designed to be at least three storeys high, a minimum height of 10 metres with dwellings on the street side. The ground floor was set to a height of 3.5 metres

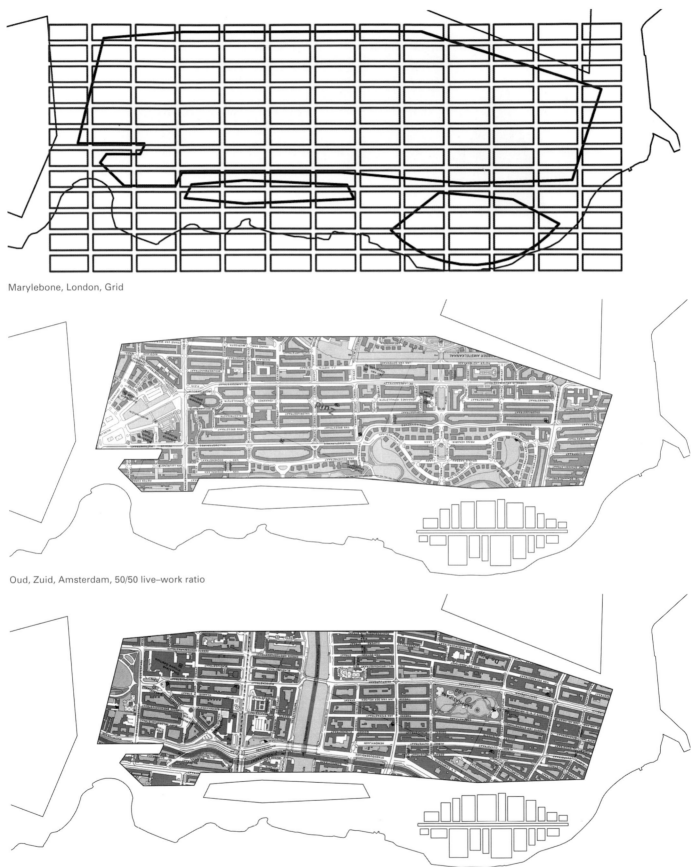

Marylebone, London, Grid

Oud, Zuid, Amsterdam, 50/50 live–work ratio

De Pijp and Oosterparkbuurt, Amsterdam, 75/50 live–work ratio

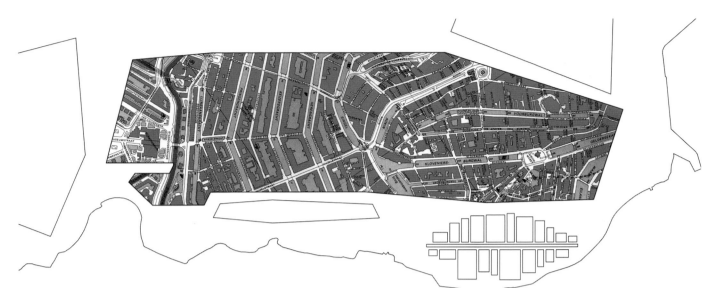

Medieval urban centre, Amsterdam, 30/70 live–work ratio

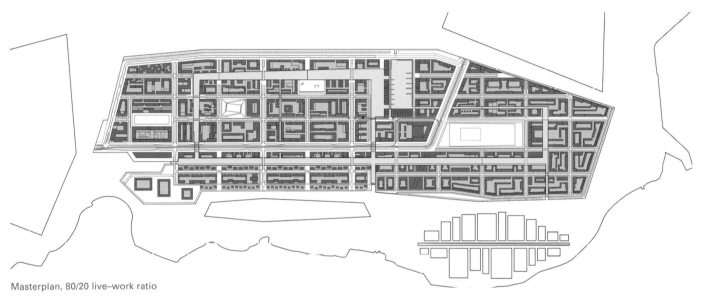

Masterplan, 80/20 live–work ratio

↖↖ Plan of the grid as proposed on Haveneiland on Ijburg. A major influence of the design and planning was the large city blocks of London's West End.

↖ Plan of Haveneiland on Ijburg superimposed as a 50/50 live–work ratio with a map of the Amsterdam neighbourhood of Oud Zuid.

← Plan of Haveneiland on Ijburg superimposed as a 75/25 live–work ratio with a map of the Amsterdam neighbourhood of De Pijp and Oosterparkbuurt.

↑↑ Plan of Haveneiland on Ijburg superimposed as a 30/70 live–work ratio with a map of the Amsterdam neighbourhood of the medieval urban centre and the seventeenth century canal rings to the south.

↑ Plan of Haveneiland on Ijburg as a 80/20 live–work ratio under the current masterplan.

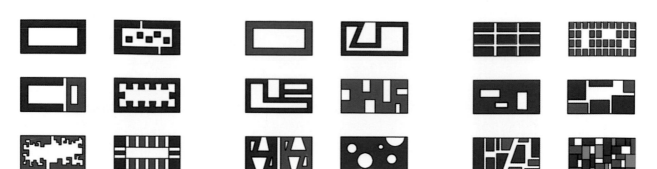

Thickening   Lengthening   Dividing

↑   Different conceptual compositional arrangements for the typical block categorised into three headings, 'thickening', 'lengthening' and 'dividing'.

↙   Axonometric section of typical terraced housing on Ijburg illustrating the relationship of the floor plan, rear gardens/courtyards and the street.

→   Large windows and skylights provide good views across the water and allow maximum light to enter the apartments.

and the first floor 2.9 metres. Each apartment block has a central void to ensure that light enters into the middle of the deep-plan accommodation.

The urban plan should offer balance between order and chaos, coherence and variety. It is intended the neutral matrix of the grid gives rise to order and variation. This was not a random decision but a carefully constructed decision after close to one hundred variants of the street pattern being considered before Felix Claus, Frits van Dongen and Ton Schaap chose the correct one. [57]

Economic functionalities, cultural diversity and social equality

There is a well-considered tenure mix comprising of an equal number of expensive and inexpensive houses and a large proportion of medium priced housing – there are 1,872 expensive dwellings, 2,496 medium-priced dwellings and 1,872 inexpensive dwellings.

There are well-connected transport links to Central Station in Amsterdam, which is 20 minutes away on the rapid tram link, and a good connection to local motorways. A large number of retail units will be constructed containing shops and restaurants, and amounting to 25 per cent of the overall development. Ijburg

has a well-considered mixture of different cultural buildings and spaces. There is a mix of play areas, crèche, sports grounds, leisure centres, a place of worship, a hotel, a doctor's practice, a riding school, a harbour and a tennis park Four large public spaces have been designed – a marketplace, a public garden, a playing field and a large city park. The urban plan also allows room for a promenade with a restaurant and landing stages for private boats.

Human scale and sustainability

On Haveneiland, the streets have been designed to be 30 metres wide from building to building, which is more than the average street in a Vinex development (22 metres wide). The pavements are 4 metres wide, generously designed to accommodate pedestrians. Parking is contained within multi-storey basements and garages within the housing blocks. The courtyards are car-free and landscaped. There is one main central avenue, which consists of rapid tram lines, a two-lane road and a bicycle lane. A four-lane motorway will be constructed close to the islands

and future development plans are in place for a bus or tram link between Almere and Amsterdam.

There is a public path along the entire perimeter of the island and there are courtyards in the middle of most blocks. The waterways are crossed by a number of bridges, such as the 6 metre high bridge to Centrumeiland in the east. On Haveneiland some houses have private gardens that border the lake. Houses can be reached by boat with a link from the private landing stages through the canals and basins to the housing blocks or private houses. There is also an inland harbour, which links Ijmeer with the inland water on Haveneiland.

A number of sustainable features have been implemented on the island. There are several parks and many new trees have been planted. Some of the individual houses have implemented many sustainable features that exceed Dutch building regulations standards.

Ijburg, Amsterdam

General

Site area	**Density**
444 hectares in total (phase 1 and 2)	60 dwellings per hectare
Haveneiland and Rieteiland islands 150.6 hectares	
Total number of inhabitants/dwellings	**Housing mix by tenure**
Currently 6,000 inhabitants. When completed 45,000 inhabitants in 18,000 dwellings	30% social housing, 70% private housing
Haveneiland and Rieteiland has 7,062 dwellings	
Average number of people per dwelling	**Percentage of commercial use**
3	25%, 490,000m² commercial and social functions
	Haveneiland and Rieteiland – 263,500m²

Spatial diversity

	Objectives	Strengths	Weaknesses	Evaluation	Design quality standard
1.	Does the scheme exploit existing buildings, landscape or topography?	Very good design around views to the sea and internal waterways.	—	Good design and planning around waterways and the sea on an artificial island.	Good
2.	Is there a variety in the types and sizes of housing?	Very good variety of housing blocks and individual houses.	—	Self-build houses have been planned around housing block.	Very good
3.	Do buildings or spaces outperform statutory minima, such as building regulations?	The design includes a very good level of detail in street design.	—	Higher ceiling heights, space standards, and street design.	Very good

Economic and social functionalities

	Objectives	Strengths	Weaknesses	Evaluation	Design quality standard
4.	Is there a mix of accommodation and community facilities that reflects the needs and aspirations of the local community?	The courtyards are car-free, quiet, sheltered, green and children can play there. Some border on the inland waterways.	—	Mix of dwellings, commercial premises and general facilities.	Good
5.	Is there a range of living, working and leisure facilities?	Very good range of living, leisure and working facilities.	—	Exemplary urban planning has included a broad range of facilities including a beach and riding school.	Very good

Cultural diversity

	Objectives	Strengths	Weaknesses	Evaluation	Design quality standard
6.	Is public space well designed and does it have suitable management arrangements in place?	Well-designed public squares.	—	Four large public spaces have been designed in the grid – a marketplace, a public garden, a playingfield and a city park.	Good
7.	Are there any technological innovations?	—	—	Good street design with wide pavements and courtyards. Good robust design of individual houses with design flair.	Good
8.	Does the housing scheme have any historical and cultural precedents?	Very good historical precedents from Amsterdam, London and the USA.	—	The design is a model in how to learn from the best housing projects and recreate successful layout, form and urban grid.	Very good

Social equality

	Objectives	Strengths	Weaknesses	Evaluation	Design quality standard
9.	Is there a tenure mix that reflects the needs of the local community?	There are ten primary schools and two colleges of secondary education.	—	There is a range of local services, general amenities, businesses and a wide range of dwelling types are to be mixed in the blocks.	Good

Sustainability

	Objectives	Strengths	Weaknesses	Evaluation	Design quality standard
10.	What design features are in place to reduce the environmental impact?	—	—	—	Average
11.	Does the master plan have a coherent sustainable plan?	—	—	—	Average

Attractiveness

	Objectives	Strengths	Weaknesses	Evaluation	Design quality standard
12.	Do buildings exhibit architectural quality?	This is a unique and different approach to housing and on the whole the majority of buildings exhibit very good architectural quality.	Some buildings are less architecturally strong, especially the older buildings with less quality.	Excellent variety in architectural design with a mixture of styles, construction process and typologies.	Very good
13.	Has the scheme made use of advances in construction or technology that enhance its performance, quality and attractiveness?	—	—	Individual housing projects have made advances in construction with innovative materials and construction processes used.	Good
14.	Does the scheme feel like a place with a distinctive character?	Individual houses provide excellent variety of character with a mix of heights, massing and typology.	Some buildings are less architecturally strong, especially the older buildings with less quality.	Good distinctive character with individual housing defining the character on six newly formed islands. The scheme is not yet completed.	Good

Human scale

	Objectives	Strengths	Weaknesses	Evaluation	Design quality standard
15.	Does the development have easy access to public transport?	Good links to the centre of Amsterdam, which is 15 minutes by tram/metro. Good links over several new bridges to the mainland.	—	All roads and surrounding development are relatively new.	Very good
16.	Are public spaces and pedestrian routes overlooked and do they feel safe?	—	—	Central street and waterways make wayfinding easy and are overlooked by housing blocks.	Good
17.	Does the scheme exploit existing buildings, landscape or topography?	Pavements are 4 metres wide with 1.2 metre transition zones between house and street.	—	Highways do not dominate but provide easy and effective links around the islands.	Good
18.	Are the streets pedestrian, cycle and vehicle friendly?	Cycle lanes have been constructed next to roads. The central square is pedestrian friendly.	—	Wheelchairs can access houses and apartments through the internal courtyards.	Good
19.	Are car parking and roads well integrated so they support the street scene and surrounding development?	Parking is well considered and integrates with the street. Most parking is under the blocks in basements and garages.	—	Some housing blocks have adjoined parking. Most parking is on street. Individual housing have off-site parking or garages.	Good
20.	Are streets defined by a coherent and well-planned layout?	Well-structured and planned design, with roads planned around one central street and waterways with smaller bridges leading to the mainland.	—	One central main road and tram linked with smaller side roads lead to a coherent whole.	Good

Vathorst, Amersfoort

Context

Vathorst is an entirely new housing development, located three kilometres from Amersfoort. Eleven thousand new houses will be constructed between 2001 and 2014 for 30,000 residents, covering an area of approximately 550 hectares. The development originates from the Fourth Memorandum of Spatial Planning, the Vinex policy, and demonstrates exemplary design quality in new housing in the Netherlands. It is a unique housing development due to innovative approaches towards design quality. This includes combining traditional housing in a 'classical' style with contemporary inventive architecture and offering a variety of housing types, forms and styles.

Vathorst consists of various neighbourhoods, each with its own distinctive character. The village of Hooglanderveen acts as the cultural heart of Vathorst, where the designers have attempted to create a 'village' character. De *Velden* (The Fields) has an extrovert, cosy, friendly village neighbourhood. Many houses have been designed in a classical style and the existing wooded banks alongside the waterways have all been preserved. At *De Laak* (The Lake) the landscape has been transformed and redesigned around existing canals so that bridges and grassy banks provide a buffer between houses. There is a pattern of waterways throughout the neighbourhood, overlooked by squares and avenues. Houses have been designed around existing dykes, with 65 per cent of the dwellings either situated along the waterside or looking out onto water. This neighbourhood is more urban and introvert than the other neighbourhoods and has few trees. The inhabitants here are typically two-income families. In *Het Lint* (The Ribbon) there are a number of spacious, low-density dwellings with many connecting cycle routes.

The Vathorst master plan was developed by the architecture and urban planning company Kuiper Compagnons and the landscape architecture and urban design firm West 8. The development is a public–private partnership between the Municipality of Amersfoort, which controls 50 per cent of the development, and five different property developers under the name of the Development Company Vathorst (OBV).

↑   Masterplan of De Laak, Vathorst by West 8 Architects.

Spatial diversity and attractiveness

A quality team was appointed to establish a framework of design quality, which defined a number of targets and methods that would allow the best quality to be enforced. The partnership contractual model that was established was a split 50/50 stake in the design and construction between the municipality of Amersfoort and five development companies. This meant the risk was jointly shared and quality was evaluated within each principal role. The master planners and the quality team sought to create a balance of contemporary housing and what they

defined as 'classical' housing, a traditional style of the classical house and contemporary housing.

The master plan sought a balanced design using different styles and architectural features. Different themes were created for each neighbourhood; for example, one block in De Laak uses a theme of water in the design, with an image of fish on its metal gates. The materials used are bold but warm – green copper façades and timber beams with large, full-height windows. Many houses have a contemporary look and offer a visual variety of form and colour.

Economic functionalities, cultural diversity and social equality

There is a diverse range of dwelling sizes in Vathorst, ranging from 100 square metres for small individual houses to 500 square metres for the higher end luxury housing. The early planning of community facilities was essential for achieving successful neighbourhoods. Vathorst has its own educational and health care facilities, and a newly constructed train station. It has a number of new cycle lanes and good facilities for cyclists.

Vathorst is bordered by a new shopping centre with retail and commercial spaces, where construction was started in 2007. In general businesses and organisations are very pleased with Vathorst, and consider it a very diverse and well-designed area.[58]

Human scale and sustainability

Within the neighbourhoods there are some successfully designed *woonerfs*, or Home Zones. A *woonerf* is a street or a group of streets where cyclists and pedestrians have legal priority over motorists. The speed limit for cars that enter a *woonerf* is equivalent to the speed of a pedestrian. The road has been designed to give maximum pavement and cycle lane widths, with a single-lane access road in the centre. Well-designed bridges cross the water and roads lead to a number of small parks. There are some private parking spaces but most parking is alongside the residential roads. Some housing blocks have rear car parking in private mews courtyards.

Vathorst has achieved a higher environmental performance than the current Dutch building regulations. The national standard is currently 1.0 Energy Performance Rating in the Netherlands, and the new development at Vathorst achieved a 0.8 Energy Performance Rating. This achievement can be attributed to the successful implementation of a quality team developing new ideas or evaluating tried and tested ideas from neighbouring housing projects, and a vigorous sustainable design process from the early master plan stage onwards. During these early

meetings, sustainability targets were developed for Vathorst relating to issues such as the use of enhanced building regulatons, embodied energy, materials, ventilation, and the environment. Sustainable features included district heating from a central incinerator and the efficient use of space. A grey water system, solar energy and a clean water sewer system were put into operation. The retention of the existing landscape was held to be of key importance and the design team went to great lengths to ensure that ditches and canals and the associated trees and shrubs were kept. Existing birds' nests were also retained within the eaves of existing houses and within hedgerows. Some ditches were made wider, from 2 metres to 20 metres, to create a natural buffer at the edge of the development. Existing roads on the site were re-used. Landscaping designers specified certain types of soil, herbs and shrubs so that birds could graze on the new grass and shrubbery. The suburb of De Laak developed a collective collection point for rubbish to minimise travel distances and implement a more efficient recycling system.

↖ A typical individual house in De Laak, Vathorst.

← Rear of new housing in De Laak with storage space, communal bins and private parking.

→ A passageway to the rear shared spaces in De Laak continues the theme of water, with the fish emblem.

Vathorst, Amersfoort

General

Site area	**Density**
560 hectares, 228 hectares for housing	Varies. 35.7 dph in De Velden, 44 dph in De Laak, 41 dph in De Bron
Total number of inhabitants/dwellings	**Housing mix by tenure**
30,000 residents, 10,632 dwellings when completed	35% social housing (60% social rent, 40% free-financed housing for people with a lower income), 32% medium priced housing, 33% expensive housing
Currently 3,500 houses constructed	
De Velden: 4,400 dwellings	
De Laak: 5,000 dwellings	
De Bron: 1,600 dwellings	
Average number of people per dwelling	**Percentage of commercial use**
2 to 3	10% (30 hectares for companies, 100,000m² for office space and 20,000 m² retail)

Spatial diversity

	Objectives	Strengths	Weaknesses	Evaluation	Design quality standard
1.	Does the scheme exploit existing buildings, landscape or topography?	Good use of existing waterways and existing landscaping.	—	Very flat site with practically no existing older buildings. Good use of waterways and parks around buildings.	Good
2.	Is there a variety in the types and sizes of housing?	—	—	Very good mix of neighbourhoods and types and sizes of housing.	Good
3.	Do buildings or spaces outperform statutory minima, such as building regulations?	—	—	The national standard is currently 1.0 Energy Performance Rating in the Netherlands. Vathorst achieved a 0.8 Energy Performance Rating.	Good

Economic and social functionalities

	Objectives	Strengths	Weaknesses	Evaluation	Design quality standard
4.	Is there a mix of accommodation and community facilities that reflects the needs and aspirations of the local community?	Good mix of community facilities and accommodation.	—	Vathorst has its own educational and health care facilities, and a newly constructed train station. It has a number of new cycle lanes and good facilities for cyclists.	Good
5.	Is there a range of living, working and leisure facilities?	—	—	It is bordered by a new shopping centre with retail and commercial spaces, which started construction in 2007.	Good

Cultural diversity

	Objectives	Strengths	Weaknesses	Evaluation	Design quality standard
6.	Is public space well designed and does it have suitable management arrangements in place?	Well-designed public spaces.	—	The management is PPP construction, a joint venture of 50% municipality operated and 50% for private partners.	Very good
7.	Are there any technological innovations?	—	—	Innovations in sustainable design.	Good
8.	Does the housing scheme have any historical and cultural precedents?	—	—	Precedents derive from local neighbourhoods Kattenbroek and Nieuweland.	Average

Social equality

	Objectives	Strengths	Weaknesses	Evaluation	Design quality standard
9.	Is there a tenure mix that reflects the needs of the local community?	Good tenure mix that is reported to reflect the needs of the local community.	—	35% social housing (60% social rent, 40% freefinanced housing for people with a lower income), medium priced houses, 33% expensive housing.	Very good

Sustainability

	Objectives	Strengths	Weaknesses	Evaluation	Design quality standard
10.	What design features are in place to reduce the environmental impact?	Sustainable features included district heating from a central incinerator and the efficient use of space. A grey water system, the use of solar energy and a clean water sewer system were all included.	—	Complies with government building regulations and policy of sustainable development. Each house has an energy performance rate of 0.8 per dwelling.	Very good
11.	Does the master plan have a coherent sustainable plan?	It includes low energy street lighting and a modern rainwater collection system. Large areas are connected to the city's district heating system	—	Good, coherent, sustainable plan.	Very good

Attractiveness

	Objectives	Strengths	Weaknesses	Evaluation	Design quality standard
12.	Do buildings exhibit architectural quality?	Excellent design of certain housing projects with good attention to detail.	—	Excellent design flair of certain housing projects.	Very good
13.	Has the scheme made use of advances in construction or technology that enhance its performance, quality and attractiveness?	Good advances in construction techniques, design and sustainable design.	—	Vathorst has achieved a higher environmental performance than the current Dutch building regulations.	Good
14.	Does the scheme feel like a place with a distinctive character?	Individual housing projects demonstrate character very successfully with good mixture and variety of housing.	—	The master plan sought a balanced design using different styles and architectural features.	Very good

Human scale

	Objectives	Strengths	Weaknesses	Evaluation	Design quality standard
15.	Does the development have easy access to public transport?	Good public transport with bus and train links.	Some housing is not reached by public transport, and reached only by car.	High-speed train link connecting the city of Utrecht. Good bus links.	Good
16.	Are public spaces and pedestrian routes overlooked and do they feel safe?	The majority of housing have been designed successfully so that roads do not dominate. Good mixture of parking.	—	The road has been designed to give maximum pavement and cycle lane widths with a single lane access road in the centre.	Good
17.	Does the scheme exploit existing buildings, landscape or topography?	There is a good balance between the roads, car parking and buildings.	—	Within the neighbourhoods there are some successfully designed *woonerfs*, or Home Zones.	Very good
18.	Are the streets pedestrian, cycle and vehicle friendly?	Good cycle routes. Cycle lanes will form a grid across the site at 500 meters apart.	—	—	Very good
19.	Are car parking and roads well integrated so they support the street scene and surrounding development?	Good integration of car parking with well-designed parking spaces. Car parking under taller apartment buildings.	Some parking in front of waterways with car dominating street scene.	Good integration of car parking with well-designed parking spaces. Car parking under taller apartment buildings.	Good
20.	Are streets defined by a coherent and well-planned layout?	For a large site it is well planned and coherent.	—	No true centre of the town, but well planned.	Good

Leidsche Rijn, Utrecht

Context

Leidsche Rijn is the largest new housing development in the Netherlands and is an example of the Dutch Vinex housing policy. The new town covers an area of 2,560 hectares and lies adjacent to the city of Utrecht. Thirty thousand new dwellings are to be constructed by 2025 with 90,000 residents in total. Twelve thousand dwellings have already been constructed; a further 2,300 are being constructed every year. There are two development phases, phase one from 1995 to 2005 and phase two from 2005 to 2015. The development was supported by the Dutch government through the Fourth National Policy, the Vinex policy. In April 1994, the municipal councils of Utrecht and Vleuten-De-Meern commissioned a single project team to draw up the master plan, appointed by the representatives of the differing disciplines and official government departments as an interdisciplinary team. Four urban design practices developed eight sectors of the master plan drawn up by Riek Bakker, the project supervisor, with the urban planner Rients Dijstra of Max.2 in collaboration with two architecture historians, Michelle Provoost and Wouter Vanstiphout.

Agreements were drawn up with the councils regarding the method of working, the public availability of the documents and the period within which the various sections of the plan would be submitted. The master plan was created to tackle the large housing shortage in and around the urban area of Utrecht with the three main themes of compactness, durability and identity. The master plan was designed to be as flexible as possible to meet unpredictable future developments as it would take 20 years to complete. Langerak was the first neighbourhood to be constructed in Leidsche Rijn. It consists of 865 low-rise row houses designed around new landscaped areas and situated next to existing canals and ditches. The urban design for the district of Langerak was based on dividing the new town into a northern strip with high densities and a southern area for low densities. A design code was then enforced to achieve a maximum of flexibility and a certain housing typology. The northern strip and southern strip had their own design code where plot sizes and building types were defined.

Spatial diversity and attractiveness

The design of the town was based on a combination of three specific elements – (1) identity; (2) closely bound; and (3) area:

↑   Masterplan of Langerak, Leidsche Rijn.

↖   Scherf 13 at Leidsche Rijn.

←   Concept sketches for Scherf 13.

→   An innovative approach to parking at
    Scherf 13.

↓   New terraced housing in Leidsche Rijn.

↘   New apartment blocks by Palmboom Van
    Den Bout Architects in Leidsche Rijn.

↑↑   An apartment block at Langerak, Leidsche Rijn.

↑   Balconies at the rear of a housing block in Langerak, Leidsche Rijn.

↗   Terraced housing, Langerak, by Maccreanor Lavington Architects.

basic elements that were implemented to make the design as flexible as possible.[59] The residential building of Scherf 13 was designed with a brief for an eight-storey apartment complex adjacent to a park. The architects SeARCH proposed that the parking zone of 100 spaces be located underneath the apartments. A car-free environment in the centre of the project was created where parking had initially been planned. There is now an open courtyard between two linear building volumes. The result is a good quality design of a large residential block with an innovative and contemporary approach.

Economic functionalities, cultural diversity and social equality

The majority of residents of Leidsche Rijn come from the surrounding villages, older suburbs and the city of Utrecht. Sixty-five per cent of the residents of Leidsche Rijn originally lived in Utrecht. Thirty per cent of new housing will be developed by the public sector and 70 per cent by the market sector.

There are two new railway stations, new cycle lanes and a new high-speed bus service, which is 15 minutes away from the centre of Utrecht. Three new bridges were constructed over the Amsterdam-Rijn canal, including The Prince Claus Bridge, designed by the architect Ben van Berkel, and they link Leidsche Rijn to Utrecht's city centre. Motorways and interlinking roads were integrated into the design, particularly the partially roofed A2 motorway.

Leidsche Rijn Centrum is a new element of the master plan and the second phase of the development of Leidsche Rijn. It will be the cultural urban heart of the new town, with new retail facilities and cinemas. The district is being designed and constructed neighbourhood-by-neighbourhood, enabling urban planners and architects to respond to future changes of urban circumstances.

Human scale and sustainability

One of the core design features of the master plan was the rerouting and partial roofing of the A2 motorway. A part of the motorway was designed with a sloping grass roof so that noise pollution could be reduced and the design of the new town

could bypass building regulations, which specify that due to noise pollution no new dwellings can be built within 600 metres of a motorway. As a result, new housing could be built right to the edge of the motorway, along with associated leisure facilities such as tennis courts and parks.

Traffic was designed to be as restricted as possible, with an average of 1.2 car parking spaces allocated for each dwelling. A green zone of public spaces, allotments and football pitches was designed to act as a buffer between the smaller neighbouring town of Vleuten-De-Meern and Leidsche Rijn. Public transport and bicycles were prioritised; cycle lanes form a grid across the site at 500 metres apart with a distinction made between smaller and larger cycle paths, some combined with road traffic routes.

There are a relatively high number of parks and landscaped areas. The master plan is based around a large green lung, the Leidsche Rijn Park, which is one of the largest city parks in the Netherlands. Sustainable design was included in the master plan with water retrieval and retention of precipitation. Investment has gone into environmental protection and energy management. There is a rainwater collection system and low energy street lighting.

Leidsche Rijn, Utrecht

General

Site area	**Density**
2560 hectares	37 dwellings per hectare
Total number of inhabitants/dwellings	**Housing mix by tenure**
30,000 dwellings, 90,000 inhabitants (proposed)	30% social and 70% private rented and privately owned
Average number of people per dwelling	**Percentage of commercial use**
2.5	700,000 m² offices, 280 gross hectares business

Spatial diversity

	Objectives	Strengths	Weaknesses	Evaluation	Design quality standard
1.	Does the scheme exploit existing buildings, landscape or topography?	Good use of existing waterways and existing landscaping.	Substantial high-speed train line in centre of site.	Very flat site with practically no existing older buildings. Good use of waterways and parks around buildings.	Good
2.	Is there a variety in the types and sizes of housing?	Good variety in types and sizes of housing.	—	The design of the town was based on a combination of three specific elements.	Good
3.	Do buildings or spaces outperform statutory minima, such as building regulations?	—	—	—	Average

Economic and social functionalities

	Objectives	Strengths	Weaknesses	Evaluation	Design quality standard
4.	Is there a mix of accommodation and community facilities that reflects the needs and aspirations of the local community?	Some community facilities provided with small individual shops and larger stores out of town.	—	The new Leidsche Rijn Centrum will provide many new retail and community facilities and cinemas when it is completed.	Good
5.	Is there a range of living, working and leisure facilities?	—	—	Leidsche Rijn Centrum is a new element of the master plan and the second phase of the development of Leidsche Rijn.	Good

Cultural diversity

	Objectives	Strengths	Weaknesses	Evaluation	Design quality standard
6.	Is public space well designed and does it have a suitable management arrangements in place?	Well-designed public spaces, mainly local authority maintained.	As the scheme is not yet completed much space between housing is still not yet built on, so undeveloped.	Good variety and mix of public space with children's playgrounds, parks and paths next to waterways.	Very good
7.	Are there any technological innovations?	One of the core design features of the master plan was the rerouting and partial recovering (roofing) of the A2 motorway	—	Housing is built right to the edge of the motorway (which has been roofed), with associated functions such as leisure facilities of tennis courts and park areas.	Good
8.	Does the housing scheme have any historical and cultural precedents?	—	—	—	Average

Social equality

	Objectives	Strengths	Weaknesses	Evaluation	Design quality standard
9.	Is there a tenure mix that reflects the needs of the local community?	The very large site provides a mix of dwellings	—	Good variety of tenure mix.	Good

Sustainability

	Objectives	Strengths	Weaknesses	Evaluation	Design quality standard
10.	What design features are in place to reduce the environmental impact?	A green zone of public spaces, allotments and football pitches.	—	Sutainability is well considered in some housing projects. Well designed for user.	Good
11.	Does the master plan have a coherent sustainable plan?	Low energy street lighting and a modern rainwater collection system have been included. Large areas are connected to the city's district heating system.	—	There are a number of parks and landscaping has been well considered. There are smaller parks and gardens linked to the larger centre park.	Good

Attractiveness

	Objectives	Strengths	Weaknesses	Evaluation	Design quality standard
12.	Do buildings exhibit architectural quality?	Excellent design of certain housing projects with good attention to detail.	Some schemes not as architecturally strong.	Excellent design flair of certain housing projects.	Good
13.	Has the scheme made use of advances in construction or technology that enhance its performance, quality and attractiveness?	Excellent attractiveness and quality of the majority of new housing schemes on the site.	Some housing less successful.	Modern, attractive and wide variety of different housing schemes.	Good
14.	Does the scheme feel like a place with a distinctive character?	Individual housing projects demonstrate character very successfully with good mixture and variety of housing.	Very large site and much still incomplete. Character lacking on some housing schemes.	Very large site and difficult to design in character. Large train link splitting site in two. Some mixed use housing.	Good

Human scale

	Objectives	Strengths	Weaknesses	Evaluation	Design quality standard
15.	Does the development have easy access to public transport?	Good public transport with bus and train links.	Some housing not reached by public transport and reached only by car.	High-speed train link connecting with the city of Utrecht. Good bus links.	Good
16.	Are public spaces and pedestrian routes overlooked and do they feel safe?	—	—	The site feels safe with many dwellings overlooking roads and parking.	Good
17.	Does the scheme exploit existing buildings, landscape or topography?	The majority of houses have been designed successfully so that roads do not dominate. Good mixture of parking.	Difficult to find one's way around	Car parking under taller apartment buildings Good design and integration of parking.	Very good
18.	Are the streets pedestrian, cycle and vehicle friendly?	Good cycle routes. Cycle lanes will form a grid across the site at 500 metres apart.	Poor for the pedestrian, lack of footpaths. Mainly vehicle orientated.	Pedestrian footpaths not well considered but good cycle routes.	Average
19.	Are car parking and roads well integrated so they support the street scene and surrounding development?	Good integration of car parking with well-designed parking spaces. Car parking under taller apartment buildings.	Some parking in front of waterways with cars dominating street scene.	Traffic designed to be limited as much as possible with an average 1.2 car parking spaces allocated for each dwelling.	Good
20.	Are streets defined by a coherent and well-planned layout?	For a very large site it is well planned and coherent.	No real heart of the new town, difficult to get around by foot.	No true centre of the town and difficult to get around but well planned.	Average

Ypenburg, The Hague

Context

Ypenburg is a new housing development situated on a former military airbase and located between The Hague and Delft. The new town consists of 12,000 new homes on 600 hectares of land. The housing development contains some excellent examples of good design quality and is a good example of housing built under the Vinex policy. The master plan, designed by the architecture firm Palmboom and Van den Bout in 1994, sought to use the existing characteristics of the site. For example, the former runway is now the broad central boulevard and the existing dykes have been reshaped into lakes and waterways.

Ypenburg is made up of five districts – De Singels, Boswijk, De Venen, Waterweld and De Bras. Each district, or 'field', has been designed with different themes to give identity and variety. All 'fields' differ in urban, architectural and landscape design within a restricted master plan. Within each district the average dwelling size varies, with 130 square meters in Waterweld and 125 square meters in De Singels. Each district also differs in density, with

14 dwellings per hectare in Boswijk, 31 dwellings per hectare in Waterweld and 48 dwellings per hectare in De Singels.

At De Singels, each dwelling is facing one of the three 'void' public spaces or is on a street that leads to one of them. The three public spaces have been given their own identity through a specific open space design. The district of Waterweld, designed by Van Sambeek, Van Schooten and MVRDV is divided into a number of 'artificial islands' with experimental housing projects. Waterwijk by MVRDV is located in the north-east section of Ypenburg and consists of a rectangular grid, each containing four dwellings with an enclosed large street wall and private gates providing access to internal patios.

There are a number of interesting projects in Ypenburg, which includes good quality housing with contemporary design. The Binnensingel subplan by West 8 landscape architects and urban planners contains mixed tenure; 631 dwellings are divided into 296 private single family houses, 104 apartments and 231 rented houses. This variety of housing types has produced a diversified appearance with staggered façade heights, controlled within a

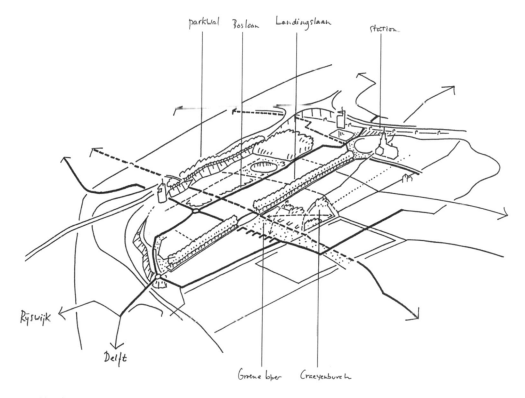

↗   Sketches of the different neighbourhoods in Ypenburg.

←   Waterwijk, Ypenburg by MVRDV Architects.

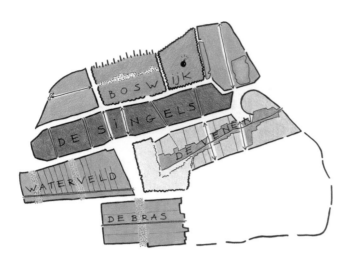

strict design code. Variety is also expressed through different floor heights, varying number of floors and differences in the direction of the roof slopes. The proposal is based on a coherent plan for the whole neighbourhood.

The land was entirely government-owned, which made it possible to design in accordance with government policy. Seventy-five groups of developers, urban planners, architects and landscape designers competed for contracts for 15 neighbourhoods for the development of 15,000 homes. There was a high design consultation and negotiation process, which made design practices strive for well-designed proposals.

↑   The five urban fields were planned on a disused airfield.

↗   Blueprint plan of new housing in Ypenburg planned on existing dykes and waterways.

↓   Ypenburg centre by Rapp & Rapp Architects.

Spatial diversity and attractiveness

The masterplanners Frits Palmboom and Els Bet chose water as a central theme for Ypenburg. Water makes up much of the development with a matrix of lakes, canals and streams. Houses are planned around these water themes and some houses sit on stilts over small lakes. In the district of De Singels, the largest district in Ypenburg with five thousand new homes, the master plan provided for many public spaces, wide, tree-lined roads, public gardens and a large urban avenue. To add urban diversity, several six-storey residential apartment blocks were constructed along the south perimeter of the district. The design teams of Ypenburg sought to learn from the mistakes of the previous Vinex schemes and as a result the design implemented a higher density with more urban character than previously found within the Vinex housing developments.

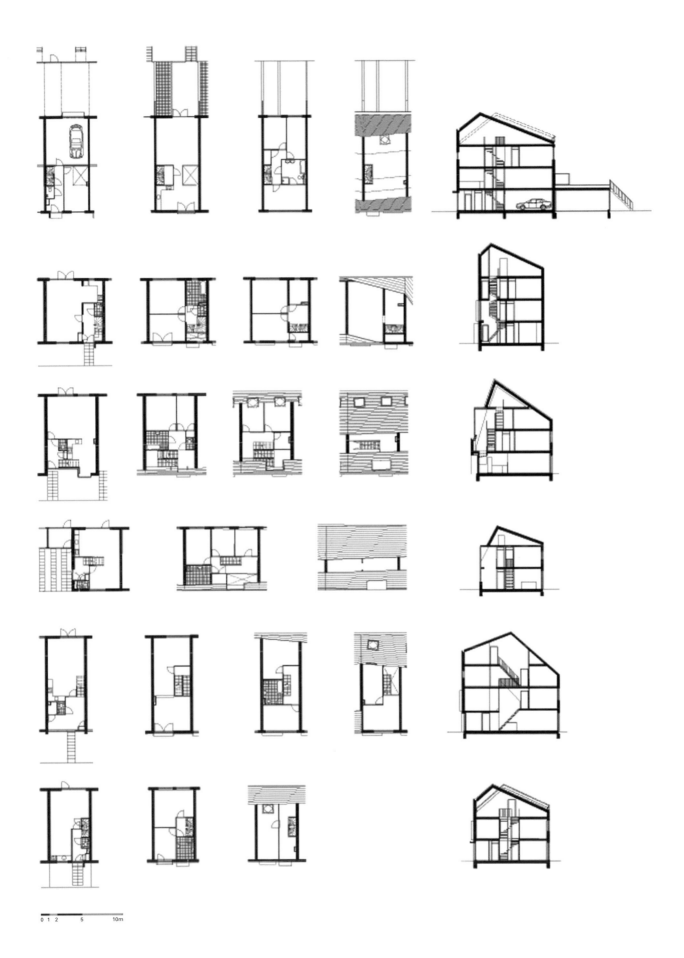

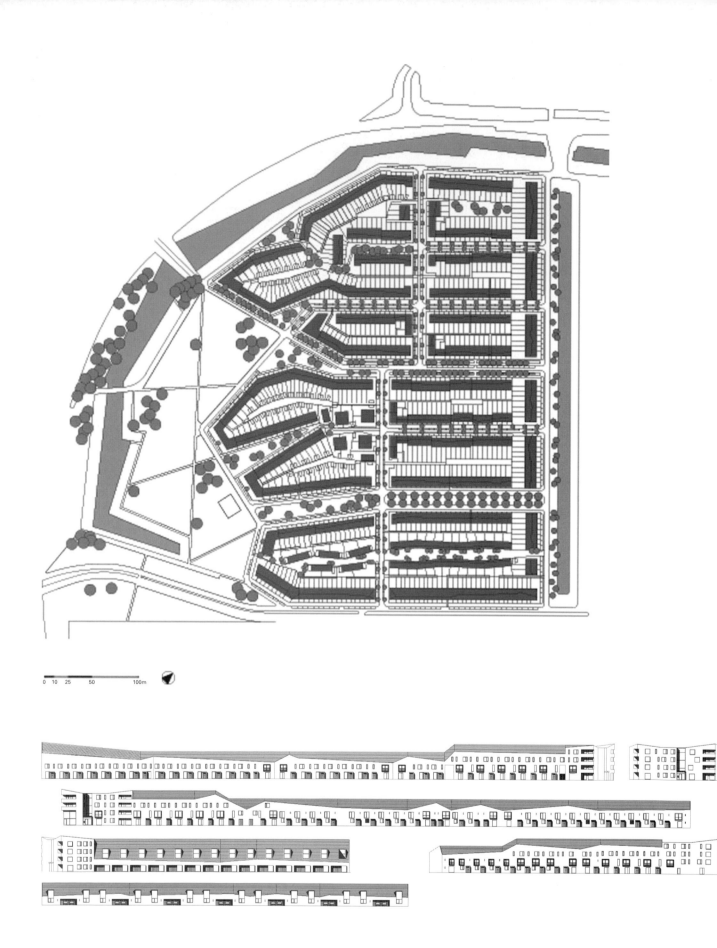

0 10 25 50 100m

←   Plan and elevations of Singels 11, Ypenburg.

↑→   Singels 11, Ypenburg.

↑   Singels 11 by Maccreanor Lavington Architects.

↓   View of the shared and public spaces of new housing Ypenburg
     planned adjacent to existing waterways.

↗   New housing overlooks the existing dykes and waterways.

The housing scheme by Dick van Gameren, which was completed in 2002, shows a mixture of housing types. The conceptual basis of the 650 homes is to create a link between the district and its surroundings. Homes are orientated towards the landscape, and greenery penetrates far into the neighbourhood. The tapered gutter and ridge lines of the roofs reinforce the dynamic of the long terraces and confer unity on the different blocks, concealing a diversity of dwelling types. A limited range of materials and colours were used for the elaboration of the façades, strengthening the continuity of the outdoor space.

The design of the Hagen Island housing scheme in Waterwijk by MVRDV achitects consists of four rows of offset housing plots. Variation is achieved by alternating the materials and colours of both roofs and façades. Four different materials are used for the pitched roofs and the façades: wood, tiles, corrugated metal and aluminium. Hedges form the borders between gardens and there are greenhouses in rear gardens.

Economic functionalities, cultural diversity and social equality

There is one central public plaza in Ypenburg, which is a hub for local trams and buses. Seven high-rise apartment blocks tower over the plaza, each containing between 12 to 18 floors. The district is well-connected by public transport; it takes 20 minutes by train and tram to reach The Hague. There are a number of shops, restaurants and retail outlets around the plaza in higher density blocks. Good road connections exist to the three surrounding motorways.

There is a good mix of tenure. Thirty per cent of the housing is affordable housing, 45 per cent has been allocated as medium priced housing and 25 per cent is luxury housing. Dwelling sizes vary between 140 square metres and 180 square metres for houses and the average size of the 192 apartments is 110 square metres. There are a number of schools, community centres, doctors' practices and a few local shopping facilities within the housing development.

Human scale and sustainability

A number of sustainable features have been implemented within the master plan. These include reusing some of the runway and the control tower of the former airport. Many new trees have been planted and the existing dykes have been shaped into waterways.

Ypenburg, The Hague

General

Site area	**Density**
600 hectares total, 340 hectares for housing	37 dph overall, 14 dph in Boswijk, 31 dph in Waterwijk and 48 dph in De Singels
De Singels 17.5 hectares	
Total number of inhabitants/dwellings	**Housing mix by tenure**
12,000 when completed, 60 per cent of dwellings have been completed	30% of the housing is affordable, 45 % has been allocated as medium priced
De Singels 652 dwellings	housing and 25% is luxury housing.
Average number of people per dwelling	**Percentage of commercial use**
2	85 hectares business park and 7,000 square meters of retail space

Spatial diversity

	Objectives	Strengths	Weaknesses	Evaluation	Design quality standard
1.	Does the scheme exploit existing buildings, landscape or topography?	The masterplan, designed by the architecture firm Palmboom and Van den Bout in 1994 sought to use the existing characteristics of the site.	—	The former runway is now the broad central boulevard and the existing dykes have been reshaped into lakes and waterways.	Very good
2.	Is there a variety in the types and sizes of housing?	Good variety of housing.	—	Good variety of housing.	Good
3.	Do buildings or spaces outperform statutory minima, such as building regulations?	—	—	—	Average

Economic and social functionalities

4.	Is there a mix of accommodation and community facilities that reflects the needs and aspirations of the local community?	Good mix of accommodation and community facilities.	—	There are a number of schools, community centres, doctors' practices and a few local shopping facilities within the housing development.	Good
5.	Is there a range of living, working and leisure facilities?	There are a number of shops, restaurants and retail outlets around the plaza in higher density blocks.	—	—	Good

Cultural diversity

6.	Is public space well designed and does it have suitable management arrangements in place?	There is one central public plaza in Ypenburg, which is a hub for local trams and buses.	—	Many public spaces with one large urban plaza in the centre of Ypenburg.	Good
7.	Are there any technological innovations?	—	—	Good architectural innovations for individual housing.	Good
8.	Does the housing scheme have any historical and cultural precedents?	—	—	—	Good

Social equality

9.	Is there a tenure mix that reflects the needs of the local community?	30% of the housing is affordable housing, 45% has been allocated as medium priced housing and 25% is luxury housing.	—	Good mix of tenure across the five districts. Dwelling size of houses varies between 140m^2 and 180m^2.	Good

Sustainability

	Objectives	Strengths	Weaknesses	Evaluation	Design quality standard
10.	What design features are in place to reduce the environmental impact?	Reusing the runway and the control tower of the former airport.	Not many sustainable features implemented.	Many new trees have been planted and the existing dykes have been shaped into waterways.	Average
11.	Does the master plan have a coherent sustainable plan?	—	—	Good use of former runway and water.	Average

Attractiveness

	Objectives	Strengths	Weaknesses	Evaluation	Design quality standard
12.	Do buildings exhibit architectural quality?	Generally good quality.	Some housing blocks have less quality.	Disproportionate level of quality in scheme. Some individual housing schemes exhibit better quality than others.	Good
13.	Has the scheme made use of advances in construction or technology that enhance its performance, quality and attractiveness?	Some individual housing developments feature advances in construction, performance and quality.	Most housing blocks have not made advances in construction or performance.	Ypenburg contains a mixture of advanced individual housing developments with a number of housing blocks that have not made any advances.	Good
14.	Does the scheme feel like a place with a distinctive character?	Individual housing projects have very good distinctive character attributes.	The central plaza lacks a sense of character.	The centre does not have as much character as individual housing schemes on the edges of Ypenburg.	Good

Human scale

	Objectives	Strengths	Weaknesses	Evaluation	Design quality standard
15.	Does the development have easy access to public transport?	Good connections to The Hague on the tram, train and bus.	—	Fast public transport network links.	Good
16.	Are public spaces and pedestrian routes overlooked and do they feel safe?	—	—	All public spaces are overlooked and feel safe.	Good
17.	Does the scheme exploit existing buildings, landscape or topography?	Good road connections exist to the three surrounding motorways.	—	There is one broad central road and a number of interconnecting roads. Roads do not dominate.	Good
18.	Are the streets pedestrian, cycle and vehicle friendly?	Good footbridges and car bridges over the many streams, dykes and water features.	—	Wide cycle lanes next to roads. Many pedestrian footpaths.	Average
19.	Are car parking and roads well integrated so they support the street scene and surrounding development?	—	There is a lack of car parking spaces within some districts.	Mainly on-street parking with some private garages.	Average
20.	Are streets defined by a coherent and well-planned layout?	There is a large, broad avenue, which sits on the site of the former runway.	—	Good interconnecting links to the surrounding motorways but some smaller roads less easy to orientate.	Average

THE STAITHS

ACCORDIA

DONNYBROOK
MILLENNIUM VILLAGE
THAMES GATEWAY

chapter two

Design quality in the United Kingdom

Context

In November 2007 Prime Minster Gordon Brown announced to the House of Commons that three million new homes would be built by 2020. This ambitious figure, equalling 250,000 new homes a year, is the result of a shortage of public and private housing and the projected large population growth of 3.6 million people in the United Kingdom by 2025. The highest projected growth will be in the south-east of England, with the prediction that London will grow by at least 800,000 more inhabitants by 2016, equivalent to a population the size of Leeds.[1] Eighty per cent of these new dwellings will be for single-person households.[2]

To tackle the increase in new housing, a new Homes and Communities Agency was announced in January 2008 to ensure a greater supply of homes. The Homes and Communities Agency will implement the delivery of housing and regeneration, bringing together the functions of English Partnerships and the Housing Corporation. A separate Planning Reform Bill will also be created to speed up planning decisions and improve measures for major infrastructure projects. Part of the British government's plan is the proposal of ten new eco-town schemes designed to be able to reach zero carbon standards. Each scheme will consist of between 5,000 and 20,000 new homes.

Design quality will be an important characteristic of these new housing developments. This chapter, therefore, summarises current policy in the United Kingdom including the £60,000 house, the Calcutt Review and the Williams Report and assesses historical measures that have had an influence on design quality in the United Kingdom.

Policy for quality in the UK

Context

Design quality has been promoted within a large number of recent policy statements on housing in the United Kingdom and has increasingly become a central feature in the government's drive for more housing. The change of government from Conservative to Labour in May 1997 resulted in the introduction of a number of new policies with reference to the quality of cities and housing in the United Kingdom, including promoting mixed used development, increasing the competitiveness of cities and preventing urban sprawl.

In the 1990s the Conservative government had highlighted principles of design quality through a number of initiatives and discussion documents. In 1994, the *Quality in Town and Country Initiative* focused on poor design quality and housing provision and poor quality of housing development, pointing out 'Quality pays. Good quality is good economics.'[3] This document emphasised the importance of mixed-use development, sustainable development, effective design guidance and the importance of increasing densities.

The Urban Task Force

In 1998, concern over estimates of future growth predictions led the government to appoint an Urban Task Force led by the architect Richard Rogers to promote high quality architecture and urban design and to place design quality at the centre of the national effort to improve British cities. The Urban Task Force published *Towards an Urban Renaissance* and presented a new vision that supported a design-led approach to urban regeneration. The Task Force argued that the poor quality of housing has lead to a migration away from the cities. The Task Force also recommended increasing the density in existing urban areas and stated that the construction and procurement of new homes in the United Kingdom should focus on increasing floor space, providing higher ceilings, optimisation of off-site construction and flexibility of building.[4] The Task Force also promoted the value of design briefs and masterplans for advancing design quality.

Sustainable communities

In February 2003, the British Government published its Sustainable Communities Plan to tackle the housing shortage and to provide affordable homes. The Sustainable Communities Plan also set out plans for several new growth areas, four in the south-east of England in the Thames Gateway, three around Stansted, Ashford and Milton Keynes, and one each in the north and the Midlands, totalling nine Housing Market Renewal Pathfinder projects.

◤ Locations of the housing case studies in the United Kingdom.

69

The Plan focused on raising design quality by providing a mix of uses and facilities in housing developments and by raising design standards. The Sustainable Communities report *Sustainable Communities: Homes for All*, published by the Office of the Deputy Prime Minister in 2005, set out new factors for delivering sustainable housing communities, proposing high-quality, mixed use, durable, flexible and adaptable buildings and the use of materials that minimise negative environmental impacts.[5] The government established the Design for Manufacture competition of constructing a home for £60,000. The government also established the design code and appointed a number of design advisors within CABE to evaluate design standards.

Planning policy

Since the Urban White Paper in 2000, the government has stated it is committed to creating better, more habitable places through the promotion of better design. Planning Policy Statement 1 emphasised the importance of good design as being integral to new housing developments in the planning system. This statement also made clear that local planning authorities should positively encourage high-quality and inclusive design. The document Circular 01/06, published in August 2006, gave further guidance on changes to the Development Control System, requiring design and access statements to accompany most types of planning applications.

In November 2006, the British government published the Planning Policy Statement 3 (PPS3), replacing Planning Policy Guidance 3: Housing (PPG3). PPS3 set out the national planning policy framework for delivering the government's housing objectives. In it, the government states that it seeks to create a wide range of high quality homes, to improve affordability and to create 'sustainable, inclusive and mixed communities'.[6] It also spells out its desire for planning authorities to consider design quality in terms of a wider environmental performance in layout, massing and density. PPS3 also places an emphasis on family homes. For the first time, the planning system is required to consider the housing needs of children, including the importance of gardens, play areas and green spaces.

Good design should contribute positively to making places better for people. Design which is inappropriate in its context, or which fails to take the opportunities available for improving the character and quality of an area and the way it functions should not be accepted.[7]

PPS3 offers a comprehensive list of seven factors against which design quality should be assessed in a new development. These design quality definitions differ from the CABE Housing Audit and Building for Life Standard. PPS3 states that a housing development:

1. Is easily accessible and well connected to public transport and community facilities and services, and is well laid out so that all the space is used efficiently, is safe, accessible and user-friendly.
2. Provides, or enables good access to, community and green and open amenity and recreational space (including play space) as well as private outdoor space such as residential gardens, patios and balconies.
3. Is well integrated with, and complements, the neighbouring buildings and the local area more generally in terms of scale, density, layout and access.
4. Facilitates the efficient use of resources, during construction and in use, and seeks to adapt to and reduce the impact of, and on, climate change.
5. Takes a design-led approach to the provision of car-parking space, that it is well-integrated with a high-quality public realm and streets that are pedestrian, cycle and vehicle friendly.
6. Creates, or enhances, a distinctive character that relates well to the surroundings and supports a sense of local pride and civic identity.
7. Provides for the retention of re-establishment of the biodiversity within residential environments.[8]

In the earlier Policy Guidance Note 3 on Housing there was only a minor reference to the improvement of design quality within planning. Design quality was instead endorsed by the companion guide to PPG3, *By Design: Better Places to Live*. The guide set out a number of references to the high quality of new developments, including a recommendation that density should be between 30 to 50 dwellings per hectare. *By Design* stated that design quality will only be raised if attention is given to 'urban design principles and approaches which underpin successful housing, not architectural treatment.'[9]

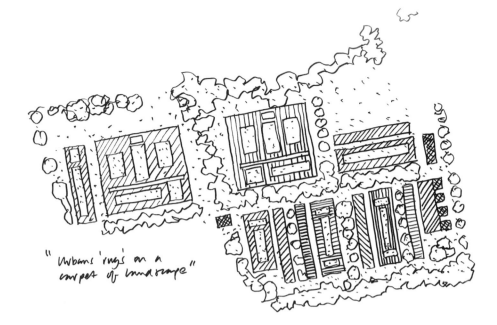

"Urbans 'rugs' on a carpet of landscape"

Commission for Architecture and the Built Environment

The Commission for Architecture and the Built Environment (CABE) is a non-departmental public body jointly funded by the Department for Culture, Media and Sport and the Department for Communities and Local Communities. It was created by the government in 1999 to raise the profile of architecture and urban design, and was given increased funding to provide greater support in delivering high-quality housing. On 6 January 2006 CABE became a statutory body under Section 87 of the Clean Neighbourhoods and Environment Act 2005. The statutory functions of CABE are set out in Section 88 of the Act and relate to the promotion, understanding and appreciation of architecture, and the design, management and maintenance of the built environment. Under Section 88 (3) (b) and Section 88 (4) (a) the Act gives CABE a specific power in providing advice and reviewing housing and building projects.

CABE claims that through public campaigns and support to professionals it can encourage better design quality. CABE states it is taking forward the design and quality agenda through the Housing Audit, the Building for Life Standard and Design Reviews. The Building for Life initiative promotes design excellence and celebrates best practice in the industry by identifying successful new housing schemes. The Building for Life Standard establishes 20 questions against which a housing scheme is assessed. On a voluntary basis, housebuilders and developers may submit their schemes for assessment against the Standard and may receive a Gold or Silver Standard award as a mark of their quality. Schemes that meet the requirement of 14 or 15 of the 20 questions are eligible to apply for a Silver Standard; schemes that meet 16 or more will be considered for a Gold Standard.

Design Review is an important part of CABE's role. There are three types of review. First, the Desktop Review, which occurs every week, where a chair of the Design Review Panel and members of CABE staff review the submitted drawings of a building project. Second, the Internal Panel Review, where schemes are reviewed by members of CABE's Design Review panel and CABE staff, in meetings that take place twice a month. Third, the Presentation Panel Review where schemes are reviewed by members of CABE's Design Review Panel and members of CABE staff. The scheme is presented by the designers and client team; other organisations, such as the local authority and English Heritage, are also invited to give their views. These meetings occur every month. CABE states it carries out Design Review assessments on around 350 schemes per year with advice from 40 experts in the Design Review Panel made up of architects, built environment professionals and designers.[10]

The 2004 CABE Housing Audit criticised the quality of new housing in the United Kingdom as being below average or poor quality. The CABE Housing Audit is a voluntary scheme and grades housing developments according to 'poor', 'average', 'good' and 'very good' characteristics. The 2004 Audit assessed contemporary design as having a trend towards *generic vernacular* architecture, 'unrelated to local building styles or materials, and with very little modern interpretation of vernacular materials or styles'.[11] The Housing Audit called for action in four priority areas to improve design quality in housing in the UK:

1. Skills – local authorities need to be better skilled so they can demand better design from the housebuilders.
2. Car parking and highways – government should replace outdated highways guidance to encourage integrated

working practices between highways engineers, urban designers and house builders.

3. Architectural design – house builders need to pay more attention to the architectural quality, the character and identity of their developments.

4. Coordination and implementation – local authorities should use the guidance on design quality that exists and be clearer about the developments they want to see; they then work with housebuilders from the outset to ensure good results are achieved.'[12]

The 2005 CABE *Housing Audit for the North East, North West and Yorkshire and Humber in the UK* concluded that poor quality is the result of poor coordination, confidence and culture. CABE evaluated three key areas of particular weakness – the legibility of new housing developments, roads and parking and a sense of place. The Housing Audit further proposed a number of recommendations to help improve better quality in new housing. These are: (1) delivering the design agenda; (2) a strategic design approach; (3) innovation in highway design; (4) creating high-quality public areas; and (5) skills and capacity.[13]

Royal Institute of British Architects

The Royal Institute of British Architects is a body for architecture and the architectural profession setting standards for the education of architects and working with the government to improve the design quality of new homes and public buildings. The RIBA argues in *Better Homes and Neighbourhoods* that minimum space standards should be introduced for all new homes, as England and Wales are the only countries in the EU that have no minimum space standards.

> The RIBA is committed to improving the design quality of UK housing. High quality housing design adds value to homes and their surroundings. It can improve the lives of residents, achieve higher values for development sites, create better public spaces and add prestige for owners... The RIBA believes that too much of the new housing stock built in the UK falls well short of the standards we should expect, in terms of both design and sustainability... But it is important to recognise that whilst architect involvement *per se* is not necessarily a guarantee of design quality, involving good designers with a wide range of expertise

is a key component of creating well-designed, sustainable and successful communities.'[14]

The RIBA also state that the challenge for architects today is to find solutions, learning from successful housing from the past whilst demanding higher standards within modern society.

The challenge for architects is to support housing providers in finding new solutions of general application – as adaptable and popular as Victorian or Georgian housing but designed to far higher performance standards while being responsive to the complexities of modern lives and of culture and social diversity.[15]

Sunand Prasad, President of the RIBA, said in the President's Inaugural Lecture that good design in the United Kingdom is implemented through: (1) client design advisors to help ensure good client side skills; (2) design champions for much-needed leadership; (3) design quality indicators and CABE's Building for Life Standard for a common language of design quality; and (4) design review panels as a growing part of the planning process.[16]

Design for London

Design for London was established in February 2007 by the Mayor of London to promote high-quality architecture and urban design in London by bringing together design expertise from the Greater London Authority, Transport for London and London Development Agency into one single body. Design for London has no statutory powers; however, it takes a lead in providing design consultation to relevant developments, policy and strategy work on behalf of the Mayor of London. This includes working with borough councils and other key partners to input into the development of area design strategies, masterplans and planning frameworks and to ensure high-quality design is delivered in relevant development and infrastructure projects. Design for London also identifies opportunities and establishes overarching design criteria for London's public realm improvement, and establishes guidance to identify key factors for the delivery of high standards of design in high-density developments.

The Williams Report

In the Williams Report, published in May 2007, the Housing Corporation and the RIBA set out a wide range of proposals to eliminate poor design quality in the UK.[17] The report stated

that local authorities in the Thames Gateway and government departments should endorse residential design guidance based on the Building for Life Standard and other existing guidance. In doing this, the report stated, this design guidance would reinforce a policy framework and the power of the local authorities would be stronger to ensure that development proposals meet the highest design quality standards. The report recommended that the Planning Inspectorate should send a stronger message to developers and local authorities to raise the quality of new housing. The report also stated that the Housing Corporation should monitor the completed quality of housing development throughout funding agreements, and should withdraw funding if homes are below design quality standards. The report also highlighted the need for more infrastructure in the Thames Gateway and also the importance of long-term management for higher density mixed communities.

The Calcutt Review

The Calcutt Review, published in April 2007, is an independent report commissioned by the British Government to review housebuilding in the United Kingdom.[18] The review acknowledges the problems behind the delivery of new housing. It highlights over-zealous planning requirements and the chronic lack of skills within local planning authorities as reasons for poor quality in the United Kingdom. It makes a number of recommendations for the quality of new housing. These recommendations include establishing an annual customer satisfaction survey of house-buyers, which should be funded by the government and run independently of any industry interest. The review suggests that the government should cease any dealings with any housebuilding firm and agency that fails to achieve a predetermined standard of customer satisfaction within two years.

The review also recommends that there should be a design review process for housebuilding, available nationwide, which will 'deliver smoother and faster planning consent for good quality schemes while exposing and disincentivising poor quality.'[19] The assessment should take the Building for Life Standard as a starting point and be expanded to make it equal for small developments and for individual buildings as well.

The Calcutt Review acknowledges that the CABE and Building for Life Standard assessment criteria are controversial and are not accepted by all in the housebuilding industry, as the standards do not cover all aspects of design quality. The review

states that at the heart of the scheme each new home should have a logbook certifying progress against building control and warranty requirements. On sale of the new home, the logbook would be handed over to the owner as a reference document and guide for construction standards and maintenance. The Review then recommends that if a scheme has passed an assessment process it should not be subject to any further objections or conditions in relation to quality imposed by the planning authority.

The Summit House

The Summit House was a government-sponsored programme to construct a house of high quality. The Summit House was designed and constructed in 14 weeks and was exhibited at the Delivering the Sustainable Communities Summit and OFFSITE conference in 2005. It was then used for developing around 20 homes at the Allerton Bywater Millennium Community near Leeds. The house was a three-storey townhouse designed to form the end terrace of a typical street. It was also designed to achieve the EcoHomes 'Excellent' standard, use 'modern methods of construction' and to be constructed on site using a steel-

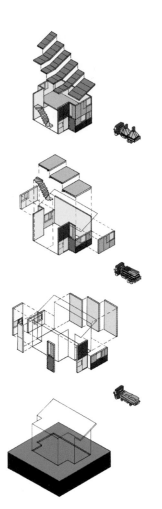

← Construction sequence drawings of the £60,000 house at Oxley Park by Rogers, Stirk and Harbour Architects.

→ Newly completed £60,000 housing at Oxley Park.

→→ Plan of the £60,000 house at Oxley Park.

↘ Construction sequence photographs of the £60,000 house at Oxley Park.

↑   The Summit House as new housing at Allerton Bywater, Leeds.

framed panelised system with a single span of 6.3 metres. The house was built to serve as a basis for a discussion forum on the summit, to trigger the development of ideas and design solutions among the participants.

The £60,000 Home

In April 2005, the then Deputy Prime Minister John Prescott announced a competition, challenging architects and developers to demonstrate that it is possible to design and build good-quality homes for a construction cost of £60,000. The competition boldly hailed itself as being a 'modern equivalent but with far greater significance for the future' of the first garden city at Letchworth Heath in 1905.[20] The competition sought to construct these £60,000 houses for large-scale housing developments that can be replicated easily and act as a catalyst for change.

The design brief placed requirements on the number of bedrooms (two bedrooms) and on the overall size of the house to at least 76.5 sq metres. Density was set to be 60 dwellings per hectare, and 30 per cent of the homes were required to be constructed for low-cost shared homeownership. The build cost of

£60,000 included builders' overheads, profits and design fees; however, the cost of site infrastructure such as estate roads, parking, gardens and drainage was not part of the construction cost target. Design statements were used for all the entries. Design codes were used to improve the quality, create consistency and speed up planning.

Oxley Park, by Rogers Stirk Harbour Architects, was the first £60,000 housing scheme to be built. The whole scheme cost £13 million and is located on a site area of 3 hectares. Fifty-six out of a total of 145 homes were constructed for the cost of £60,000. Each house was constructed in 24 hours, taking a month to build the entire scheme. Rogers Stirk Harbour Architects developed a generic house type using 'modern methods of construction', which was manufactured off-site and then transported to site for assembly. These standardised homes included specially designed 'EcoHats', which optimise energy consumption by re-using air circulating through the stack and by implementing a passive solar heating system. Through the use of different types of external cladding, several different housing varieties were designed, providing a mixture in colour and scale.

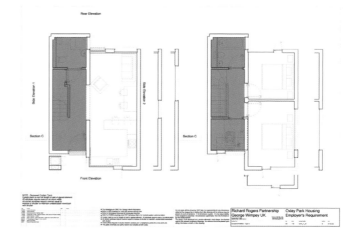

The BoKlok Home

BoKlok means 'Live Smart' in English and is marketed to be a new concept in housing that aims to provide functional and good-quality housing at an affordable price for first-time buyers, young professionals and families. BoKloK was first established in Scandinavia by the furniture company IKEA and the construction firm Skanska joining together to create a joint venture company. The UK range of housing consists of two-bedroom flats and two- and three-bedroom houses.

The typical BoKlok floor arrangement is an L-shaped, two-storey block with three apartments on each floor or as a single house. The BoKlok houses have an open-plan layout with high ceilings and large windows. They are constructed with fitted Ikea kitchens, bathrooms and a laminated timber floor. All the interior decoration and soft furnishings have been selected from IKEA's current product range and people who buy a BoKlok property will receive a £250 IKEA voucher to help them begin furnishing their home.

They have been designed to meet or exceed all building regulations, as well as being designed to have an Eco-Homes 'excellent' rating. The company's first scheme, in St James Village in Gateshead of 60 homes, was assembled from flat panels made in a factory in Milton Keynes. There are further BoKlok developments planned within the UK, including a further 100 homes in the Hendon area of Sunderland.

BRE OFFSITE 2007 Exhibition

The BRE OFFSITE 2007 exhibition opened on 11 June 2007 at the BRE centre in Watford to examine and promote new approaches to sustainable new housing and modern methods of construction that achieve higher levels of performance compared with conventional construction forms.

The exhibition showcased a range of off-site construction techniques and six construction companies erected full-size buildings that met Level 4 of the Code for Sustainable Homes, with some houses achieving Level 6 of the Code for Sustainable Homes. All the OFFSITE 2007 houses were designed and built by manufacturers and construction companies in collaboration with architects and engineers.

↑   View of new sustainable housing prototypes at the BRE OFFSITE 2007 exhibition.

→   New housing at the BRE OFFSITE 2007 exhibition.

	2002	2005	2006
Proportion of dwellings built on brownfield sites (including conversions)	67%	77%	74%
Density of new dwellings (dwellings per hectare)	27	40	41

Source: Adapted from Housing and Planning Key Facts, Analytical Services Directorate, October 2007.

Density

Density is the ratio between the number of people or house-holds and the area of land they occupy. It is usually defined by the number of dwellings per hectare or by the number of habitable rooms of a building. Historically, various cities in the UK have been developed at a wide range of densities with some successful neighbourhoods being built at relatively high densities. However, pressure on housing and concern about the long-term sustainability of large schemes containing small apartments has recently led to the development of even higher density schemes.[21]

Matthew Carmona argues that increasing the design quality of housing combined with planning requirements that influence higher residential densities is one of the major subjects of debate in our time.[22] The Design for London publication *Superdensity* highlights that higher density is vital in good quality design and good for cities generally as it encourages mixed communities, increases the economic wealth of a city and is more sustainable.[23]

> The attributes of higher density appear to fit well with the principles of good housing design. Higher density addresses the principle of car dominance; it appears to be inherently sustainable; it may promote a mixing of uses as homes, services and employment are brought closer together. It may also help nurture a sense of pace and a sense of community as people find social interaction is not hindered by the barrier of physical distance. High density, if coupled with better design, also holds the promise of more secure and safer places to live.[24]

Policy is generally moving towards higher density living as it is recognised by the government as being crucial to sustaining local facilities and services and promoting urban vitality. Changes in density levels have been implemented through the Planning Policy Guidance 3 (PPG3), which endorses urban development at higher densities by directing planning authorities to waive limits set in Unitary Development Plans. These changes will be key factors in shaping housing developments in the future and determining good design quality. The British

↑   High density housing at the Eastern Harbour District.

↗   New housing at Abbotts Wharf by Jestico and Whiles Architects.

government and the Mayor for London define high density as 60 dwellings per hectare and above, whilst medium density is defined as 30 dwellings per hectare. Planning Policy Guidance 3 stated that new housing developments should aim for a density of not less than 30 dwellings per hectare to avoid inefficient use of land.

Other parties have also endorsed higher densities. These include the Campaign to Protect Rural England, which recommends an average density of 90 dwellings per hectare for new housing in urban areas. The publication *Recommendations for Living at Superdensity* highlights that successful new housing schemes should be designed between 150 dwellings per hectare to 500 dwellings per hectare. The London Housing Federation's publication *Higher Density Housing for Families* defines higher density housing at more than 80 dwellings per hectare while the East Thames Housing Group, which has published a web-based density *toolkit*, defines higher density as over 70 dwellings per hectare.[25] The Greater London Authority, on the other hand, states that densities between 30–150 dwellings per hectare should be achieved.

We must not put quantity before quality. We must provide future generations of Londoners with the best of contemporary housing, creating places that will accommodate and sustain London's vibrant and diverse communities. High quality design and increased densities are critical to this equation...to reduce pressure on space in London we need to ensure that all new housing is built at suitable densities, which means higher densities in areas which are close to public transport and well supported by social amenities.[26]

The Commission for Architecture and the Built Environment has identified key features of successful higher density housing developments. These are good, sound insulation between dwellings, relationship with the surrounding area in terms of connectivity, scale and integration, proximity to good public transport, priority for pedestrians and cyclists, high quality open spaces to provide visual relief and recreation, some usable private outside space, clear demarcation between public and private spaces and adequate level of car parking that does not dominate the street scene.[27]

The drive for higher densities, however, does not necessarily equate to higher quality housing. Gallent and Tewdwr Jones in *Decent Homes for All: Planning's Evolving Role in Housing Provision*, argue that the drive for higher densities is a result of the philosophy 'high density good, low density bad', followed by the government.[28] As the case studies in this book illustrate low density housing can be appropriate and sensitive to the context of the site and provide as good quality housing than housing of higher densities.

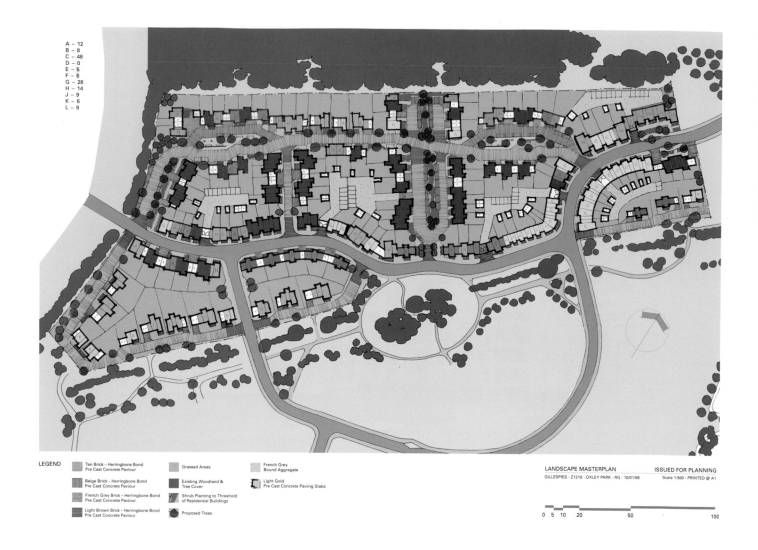

A – 12
B – 8
C – 48
D – 0
E – 5
F – 6
G – 28
H – 14
J – 9
K – 6
L – 9

LEGEND

Tan Brick – Herringbone Bond Pre Cast Concrete Paviour

Beige Brick – Herringbone Bond Pre Cast Concrete Paviour

French Grey Brick – Herringbone Bond Pre Cast Concrete Paviour

Light Brown Brick – Herringbone Bond Pre Cast Concrete Paviour

Grassed Areas

Existing Woodland & Tree Cover

Shrub Planting to Threshold of Residential Buildings

Proposed Trees

French Grey Bound Aggregate

Light Gold Pre Cast Concrete Paving Slabs

LANDSCAPE MASTERPLAN   ISSUED FOR PLANNING

GILLESPIES · Z1210 · OXLEY PARK · RG · 10/01/06   Scale 1:500 · PRINTED @ A1

0 5 10 20   50   100

Design codes

A 'design code' is a coordinating tool, which, it is claimed, facilitates the delivery of design quality. The idea behind the design code is to provide clarity over what is acceptable design for a site and thereby to provide a level of certainty for the various parties engaged in the design and planning process including developers, stakeholders and the local community. The British government is increasingly seeing the delivery of design quality through the use of the design code. This is highlighted by the government report, *Design Coding: Testing its Use in England*, launched in May 2004 to accelerate the delivery of good-quality new housing development[29] and the Planning Policy Statement 3 (PPS3), which states that high-quality design results from the use of design codes:

> To facilitate efficient delivery of high quality development, Local Planning Authorities should draw on relevant guidance and standards and promote the use of appropriate

tools and techniques, such as Design Coding alongside urban design guidelines, detailed master plans, village design statements, site briefs and community participation techniques.[30]

Historically, design codes have been used to set standards to improve health and sanitation in a number of large-scale housing developments, including the Regency terraces of London, Bath, Hove and Edinburgh. Following the great fire of London in 1666, the 1667 Act for the Rebuilding of the City of London established a typology of streets and matching buildings, materials, ceiling heights, structural requirements and regulations that led to paved, straightened streets with buildings of uniform height.

It is reported that there is a considerable interest in design codes. However, opinions on its use vary. Almost all the respondents in the survey conducted by Matthew Carmona on design coding felt that design codes can help deliver better quality design because they set minimum standards.[31] Many respondents argued that design coding can help deliver quality but can also

←←   Landscape masterplan of Oxley Park by Rogers, Stirk and Harbour Architects.

←   Design codes were used at the Greenwich Millennium Village.

for different districts, as established by the planning department in Amersfoort. Design codes were also a key component for the design of the Greenwich Millennium Village to ensure the vision of the master plan was realised through a legal agreement between the landowner and developer. The design of the Greenwich Millennium Village used the code in early stages of negotiations with the London Borough of Greenwich Planning department. English Partnerships saw the code as a way of evaluating strategic design issues.[35] The Greenwich Millennium Village code focused on building massing and the public realm but did not include any guidance on materials or detailed design of buildings.[36] However, Matthew Carmona argues that although the aim for the Greenwich Millennium Village was to create an urban character, the development has acquired a suburban character and as a consequence there are urban design problems in relation to streets and spaces. Further, Carmona argues that although the code reflected the architect Ralph Erskine's design philosophy there were conflicts between the design code's desire for hierarchy of spaces and the technical requirements of prefabrication. Also there was no reference to an established palette of colours and materials.[37]

stifle innovation and should not be used to dictate the design and aesthetical composure of a housing development because they were felt to suffocate the creativity of designers as they are excessively bureaucratic and prescriptive.[32] The lack of local authority staff time, skills and experience in the preparation of design codes was also held to be a negative factor of design codes. CABE, as a result, highlighted that there is a sense of unease among built environment professionals about the consequences design codes may have on design. 'There is a nervousness that design coding will bring a level of prescription that will stifle design creativity.'[33]

Design codes can be used to provide a useful guide to massing, block layout, street design and building performance. Codes provide a positive statement about the particular qualities of a place. The potential benefits of design codes have been stated to include a better designed development, an enhanced economic value, a more certain planning process and a more coordinated development.[34]

Today, design codes are used in a number of new housing developments. In Borneo-Sporenburg in Amsterdam, design codes were successfully used and they formed a key component in the control of development through the planning system. There were design codes for streetscape, parking, private open space, storey height and plot width. Two design codes were applied in Vathorst, a code for the overall masterplan and a code

Sustainability

'We don't want to build *more* homes. We want them to be *better* homes, built to high standards, both in terms of design and environmental impact and homes that are part of mixed communities with good local facilities...Our aim is to eliminate poorly designed new housing, and make good and very good new development the norm. And we recognise getting the design right can improve the quality of life for all members of the community, as well as improving the environment, creating safer and stronger communities and reducing our carbon footprint.[38]

In December 2006 Chancellor of the Exchequer Gordon Brown announced the British government's 'green package' with a Code for Sustainable Homes, the draft Planning Policy Statement on Climate Change and the new draft Climate Change Bill. The government announced in the housing green paper that all new homes will be zero carbon by 2016 and the proposal for ten new eco-towns.

	2010	2013	2016
Carbon improvement as compared to Part L (BRs 2006)	25%	44%	Zero carbon
Equivalent energy/carbon standard in the code	Code level 3	Code level 4	Code level 6

The Code for Sustainable Homes is an assessment rating standard for sustainable design and construction of new housing. The code measures the sustainability of a home against design categories indicated by stars. It introduces minimum standards in nine key areas including energy and water. It sets different levels of energy efficiency for buildings from one to six stars depending on the extent to which it has achieved the Code for Sustainable Home standards. One star is the entry level above the level of the Building Regulations and six stars is the highest level, reflecting exemplary development in sustainability terms. This code is in addition to the British Research Establishment EcoHomes standard, which was established in 2000 as an independent and voluntary measurement of the environmental impact of housing developments, based on the existing BREEAM scheme for commercial buildings. This assessment looks at issues related to energy, transport, pollution, materials, water, land use and ecology, health and well-being. Weighted scores are given and a rating of pass, good, very good or excellent.

The British government has set out a proposed timescale for increasing the impact of the Code for Sustainable Homes within the Building Regulations framework. For the private market, the government proposes to achieve a zero carbon goal in three steps: Code Level 3 will commence in 2010, moving to a 25 per cent improvement in the energy/carbon performance set in building regulations, rising to Code Level 4 in 2013, moving to a 44 per cent improvement, and concluding in zero carbon Code Level 6 in 2016. The strategy for delivering these targets involves changes to the Building Regulations to strengthen the requirements for various aspects such as insulation, ventilation, airtightness, heating and light fittings.

A further initiative by the government is the Carbon Challenge, which was launched in February 2007 to help accelerate the response to climate change and trial the Code for Sustainable Homes. Phase one of the challenge will focus on delivering over 1,000 homes on a minimum of five sites with two further phases to follow. The first two sites in Bristol and Peterborough will start construction in 2008.

The government is also introducing ten new eco-towns, which will act as 'exemplar green developments' of between 5,000 and 20,000 new homes. It promised to deliver new housing at higher levels than standard building regulations to maximise resource saving, including zero carbon development, achieve distinct identities, 30 to 50 per cent of affordable housing and

↑   The design of Accordia outperforms building regulations.

→   The dynamic form of the Lighthouse – the design of the Lighthouse resembles an upturned barn and is a net zero-carbon house that also meets Level 6 of the Code for Sustainable Homes.

integrated services and transport. The eco-towns will be small new towns and are intended to be of the best new architecture and to achieve zero carbon development of level five or six of the Code for Sustainable Homes. The new eco-towns draw on the thinking of urban theorists such as Ebenezer Howard and planning for the garden cities that combined 'the health of the country with the comforts of the town'.[39] There will be design competitions for key stages as quality is encouraged through a CABE-run Eco-towns Design Review Panel. The government will work with the RIBA, CABE and the Prince's Trust to stimulate new architectural thinking in design competitions.

> We will encourage the highest quality through a CABE-run Eco-towns Design Review Panel. Government will work with RIBA, CABE and the Prince's Trust to stimulate new architectural thinking, including a design competition on how to achieve a strong vision and identity in a range of illustrative new settlement types, while relating effectively to local character and reference.[40]

The Lighthouse

The Lighthouse is the UK's first net zero-carbon house that also meets Level 6 of the Code for Sustainable Homes. It was developed and constructed by Kingspan in collaboration with Sheppard Robson Architects. The design resembles an upturned barn with a 40 degree roof with two bedrooms over two and a half storeys and an internal area of 93 square metres. The living space on the first floor attempts to maximise daylight and volume, with a top-lit double height living space. Shading to the west elevation is provided by retractable shutters restricting direct sunlight, minimising heat gain in the summer. These can be folded away when not required to shade the space from evening sun.

The Lighthouse is constructed using Kingspan Off-Site's TEK Building System, a high-performance SIPS (structurally insulated panel based system), which, for the Lighthouse, will provide a high level of thermal insulation and performance – U values of 0.11W/m²K and airtightness of less than 1.0m³/hr/m² at 50Pa – reducing the heat loss by potentially two-thirds of a standard house. The foundations consist of offsite timber floor cassettes on a ring beam of timber beams supported off the ground level by screw fast pile heads.

The wind catcher, located on the roof, provides passive cooling and ventilation. When open the catcher catches the cold air, dispersing the hot air, allowing it to escape. The wind catcher also brings daylight into the house and provides the

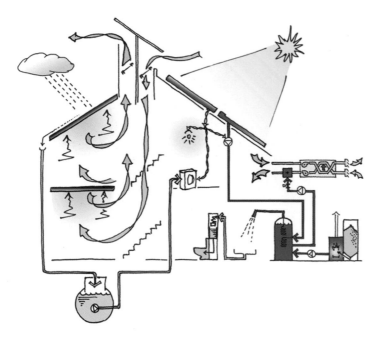

Water efficiency techniques that have been included in the Lighthouse design include low-volume, water-efficient sanitary ware and appliances, such as spray taps, a dual-flush toilet, low-flow showers and a small bath. Water from the shower and bath is recycled via a standalone grey water system that fits behind the toilet and supplies water for flushing. Rainwater from the roof is collected in a below-ground tank in the garden, which is filtered by a rainwater harvesting system and re-used by the washing machine and for watering the garden.

ground floor sleeping accommodation with secure night-time ventilation.

Renewable energy is provided by a biomass boiler with an automatic feed system for heating, building integrated photovoltaics (BIPV) electricity and a solar-thermal array, which supplies hot water and allows the boiler to be turned off in the summer and turned down in the spring and autumn, significantly reducing fuel consumption.

RuralZED home

RuralZED, designed by the architect Bill Dunster of ZEDfactory, is a new low- to medium-density zero-carbon housing concept with a variety of flats, townhouses and terraced three bedroom homes. RuralZED has been designed to exceed the standards set by the code for sustainable homes. It sets a new industry standard with a range of specification options offered from Code 3 to Code 7.

↙ The RuralZED house provides an array of photovoltaic panels on the roof, solar shading, solar thermal hotwater with woodchip back up, securely ventilated sunspace, optional wind cowls achieving passive heat recovery ventilation, AAA rated appliances and an airtight super insulated envelope.

→ The interior of the RuralZED house uses a glulam timber, which can be rapidly erected and designed simplistically to provide a choice of add-on components such as a sunspace, a choice of roof forms and a gable end wall or party wall for forming terraces.

→ The community was central to the Staiths design. There are a number of children's play areas, and games such as table tennis and community barbeques.

The houses use a flat-pack timber-frame kit that is laminated and built in a box shape formed by posts and beams on a low-carbon concrete foundation. Heavyweight eco-concrete panels manufactured using a high level of recycled aggregate content rest on the solid timber beams. These are an energy-efficient alternative to domestic plasterboard and give the house its 'thermal mass' that absorbs and releases heat slowly.

All homes have south-facing photovoltaic panels located on the roof to meet most households' annual electric demand, with solar thermal collectors and shared wood pellet boilers providing renewable warmth. Each home has one parking space, with access to a communal electric and vegetable oil car pool placed under solar electric canopies in the central mews. Central mews properties encourage people to live and work on site, with options to convert integral garages into studio space. Each home can have its own micro wind turbine, photovoltaic installation and solar thermal panels serving its own hot water store.

A true Cinderella: skills and training in the United Kingdom

If the shortages of skills are not properly addressed as a matter of urgency it is increasingly likely that we will end up with a large number of badly built houses in poorly designed communities with limited transport infrastructure that have severe environmental impacts, rather than the 'sustainable communities' that are the government's stated aim.[41]

Good housing is reliant on the training and skills of those people involved in implementing and endorsing design quality. A number of reports have emphasised the relationship between the lack of skills and training and that of design quality in housing. The lack of design skills was highlighted in the 1994 discussion document *Quality in Town and Country*.[42] This report stated that better design quality is dependent on an investment in design skills for those professionals involved in the built environment. In 1998, John Egan was commissioned by the British government to increase efficiency in the construction industry. The report *Rethinking Construction* set a number of recommendations and targets for training and skills and included the improvement of skills in construction practices.[43]

In April 2003, in response to the main recommendation of *Rethinking Construction*, Sir John Egan was asked by Deputy Prime Minister John Prescott to review the skills and training required to deliver sustainable communities. Sir John Egan's 2004 report *The Egan Review: Skills for Sustainable Communities* contained 24 recommendations, including establishing a new National Centre for Sustainable Community Skills.[44] *The Egan Review* concluded that the lack of skills amongst built environment professionals has the potential to hamper the ability of the government and housing organisations to deliver the Sustainable Communities Programme and the design quality of housing.

Design skills of staff in local authorities and the government have been criticised for contributing to poor housing quality. The CABE Housing Audit, in 2004, concluded that the skills of developers and of local authorities are critical in delivering high-quality housing, and urged developers to strengthen their teams, to appoint design champions whenever possible and to make use of the design review panels operated by CABE. The Home Builders Federation's Calcutt Review recommended that local authorities should invest in multi-disciplinary strategic teams within planning departments to discuss the design of new housing prior to planning approval. The Calcutt Review also stated that, to achieve good design quality, the roles and responsibilities of the public and private sector have to be redefined and design teams should be appointed on the basis of their skills and experience, not just the lowest bid.

Housing design must be dealt with in a more professional, rational and consistent manner within the planning system. We want to see a planning system where planners are not only well-resourced and well-trained in design matters but are also encouraged to seek expert advice from local and regional design panels where developers and design teams can engage positively with local planning authorities.[45]

→   The Greenwich Millennium Village.

The CABE report *Building Sustainable Communities: Developing the Skills we Need* has highlighted that there are a number of key areas where skills are lacking, such as skills for strategic planning, urban design, project management, and expertise in project appraisal.[46]

Planning departments and private consultancies cannot find enough good people with the necessary design skills to provide the expected level of service, and some of the basic professions are suffering falling numbers of graduates also. Everyone is talking about it but nobody wanting to do it, a true Cinderella.[47]

Design quality in the UK

Context

The quality of housing design in the UK has many historical precedents. Twentieth century changes in design quality were the result of public health and by-law requirements, which set basic standards for housing in space and access, growth of a national infrastructure such as sewage, railways, philanthropic schemes such as the Peabody Trust and housing provision by councils.[48]

Ebenezer Howard believed in the merits of design quality and in his influential book *Garden Cities of Tomorrow* sated that a new type of settlement, the garden city, could combine all the advantages of the town with that of the country through the three 'magnets' of living. Howard sought to create new towns, surrounded by a large green belt, with a residential density of 37 dwellings per hectare, outside of the commuter range of a larger city and with a relatively small population of 30,000 people. Howard believed that this size of town should be fixed and once the town's population had exceeded its population limit another new town could be created.[49]

Howard was instrumental in the birth of Port Sunlight and Bournville, which later influenced the new towns of Letchworth Garden City and Hampstead Garden Suburb. Port Sunlight was built in 1888 on the banks of the Mersey near Birkenhead, and Bournville was built in 1895 outside Birmingham with a large central green and houses reviving the character of a village. Hampstead Garden Suburb was designed by the architects Raymond Unwin and Robert Parker with the consultant architect Edwin Lutyens. Unwin regarded the quality of housing as the main criterion of planning[50] and saw Hampstead Garden Suburb as a place for everyone, with gardens and open spaces and other amenities for both the working class and other social classes.[51]

The Hampstead Garden Suburb Act of 1906 included a number of important provisions regarding density, regulations and design. This Act was passed before the first Town Planning Act 1909, to overcome local inflexible by-laws, and established important design requirements, the results of which can be seen today. Each house had to include a living room of 144 square feet (43 square metres) and one bedroom of not less than 135 square feet (41 square metres). The Act also allowed the architects to fix an average residential density of eight houses per acre (3 houses per hectare), which had a significant effect on the design of the layout. In the design advice certain materials were recommended, such as red brick, stone or roughcast as well as red roofing tiles as materials for external walls, giving the suburb a unique architectural quality.

Successful design quality in Hampstead Garden Suburb was achieved by the careful combination of design elements such as short terraces, urban courtyards, village greens and picturesque streets and the incorporation of existing landscape and trees into the design. Attention was paid to roads and paving as well as vistas and views, with vantage points of road junctions and focal buildings. Houses were allocated to various groups, each of them with different types and sizes of dwellings.

The ambitions of the garden cities led to good design quality. Many of these ideals were lost, however, to the later developments of mass housing estates in a drive for quantity after World War II.

Internal floor area (m²) as established by the Parker Morris Committee

Dwelling type	1 person	2 persons	3 persons	4 persons	5 persons	6 persons
Flat	29.7	44.6	56.7	69.7	79.0	86.4
Maisonette				71.5	81.8	91.9
Single storey house	29.7	44.6	56.7	66.9	75.3	83.6
2 storey semi or end				71.5	81.8	91.9
2 storey centre terrace				74.3	84.5	91.9
3 storey house					93.8	97.5

Design guides

An early report to implement new methods of quality control in new housing was developed in the Essex Design Guide. In 1973, Essex County Council set a framework to achieve quality in design as it was concerned with the poor visual quality of monotonous new housing being constructed in Essex. The Essex Design Guide was the first design guide in the UK and had a profound influence on housing design by other local authorities, which produced similar guides. The guide endorsed an average density of 60 and 75 dwellings per hectare and sought space standards to meet Parker Morris Standards with attention paid to privacy, use of daylight and sound insulation. The guide highlighted the need for variety. It stated that spaces should be defined by houses or trees, and designed for pedestrians. A minimum size for private gardens was set at 100 square metres.

A significant part of the guide was the requirement to design buildings to fit with the existing urban fabric. The county council took the view that where new residential development was taking place, builders and designers should attempt to heighten the building character of the country and re-establish local identity. Housing should also be designed to use external materials that are sympathetic in colour and texture to the vernacular range of Essex materials.[52] The guide led to tighter street layouts and the use of vernacular materials and building techniques. It recommended the use of the 'mews court' with a combined access area for vehicles and pedestrians. This was an attempt to move away from the car-dominated suburban layouts.

The publication provoked a response from architects, who argued that planners who were involving themselves in the aesthetics of design were stepping beyond their professional disciplines. The letters page of the *Architects Journal* featured many criticisms of the guide, as it was argued it would strangle creativity with detailed prescriptions of building façades and materials.[53] Today, however, the guide is seen by many built environment professionals to enhance the quality of housing design.

A history of space standards

Influenced by Ebenezer Howard's ideas on typical unit sizes of the garden city, the Housing Act 1919 established a guideline for minimum space standards and densities of new housing based on dimensions established within the garden cities. This Act also enacted the recommendations of the Tudor Walters report, which was commissioned by the government to review housing conditions at the end of World War I. The Tudor Walters requirements endorsed a minimum room provision of at least three ground floor rooms and three bedrooms per home, with a density of 12 dwellings per acre, built as semi-detached houses or short terraces with front and rear gardens.

After World War II there was extreme housing shortage in the UK, and a scarcity of building materials and quantity meant large numbers of prefabricated and non-traditional housing was constructed. Some commentators criticised the large areas of monotonous housing being built. Raymond Unwin in the *Design Guide* attacked the 'characterless' suburbs with the bland approach to residential and highway design.[54] In 1955, Ian Nairn in his book *Outrage* criticised the quality of standard houses and street features constructed in the UK and the failure to consider the context of the surroundings. Nairn argued that the new housing developments looked as though they could be built anywhere and had no identity or sense of place.[55]

In 1961, the Ministry of Housing and Local Government with the Central Housing Advisory Committee of London County Council launched an enquiry into development standards under the direction of Sir Parker Morris. The Parker Morris Committee drew up the seminal report for housing space standards in public housing, entitled *Homes for Today and Tomorrow*. The committee highlighted the need for space storage and for all rooms in the house to be heated. Internal floor areas were established as set out in the table above.

The report concluded that the quality of social housing needed to be improved to match the rise in living standards and made a number of recommendations. The report also emphasised the

← A communal table tennis table and courtyard at the Staiths.

need for greater flexibility in the design of housing to accommodate increases in living standards in the future. It recommended increasing floor space and reducing the number of built-in cupboards for kitchens.

> With the numerous examples in the local authority field and the best examples in the private sector there is no longer any reason why our town and countryside should continue to be spoilt by unimaginative buildings. Good layout and landscaping, together with the use of good and well chosen external materials and colours throughout an estate, go nine-tenths of the way towards creating beauty instead of ugliness, and it is in these broad and not necessarily costly ways, rather than in the laboured detailing of the individual dwelling, that housing development can be made pleasing and attractive to the eye.[56]

It was not until a few years later, however, that the impact of the Parker Morris Report was felt and only much later, in 1969, did it become mandatory for both private housing and social housing. Among the conclusions of the publication was that for houses of up to three bedrooms there should be at least one toilet and that there should be heating systems for the kitchen and other rooms in the house. It can be argued that the Parker Morris Report led to many houses that failed to meet its standards being pulled down. Criticism arose about the demolition of swathes of older housing in cities, such as eighteenth-century Georgian terraces in Liverpool, because they were considered to be sub-standard.

The mandatory enforcement of the Parker Morris Standards was abolished in 1981 after it no longer formed the basis for obtaining funding for public or housing association housing. This report is today still the most commonly cited benchmark for space standards. Parker Morris Standards are still used as a guideline for areas of new housing but no longer have any statutory weight and many houses built today no longer meet Parker

Morris Standards. Karn and Sheridan[57] identified in their research that new private and public housing is built to typical unit areas 5 per cent to 15 per cent below Parker Morris Standards.

In the 1980s, concerned with the quality of housing in the UK, the Joseph Rowntree Foundation introduced 16 criteria for the design of new housing, known as the *Lifetime Homes* standard. The Joseph Rowntree Foundation commissioned the National Housing Federation to develop a detailed series of space standards, which resulted in the National Housing Federation's *Guide to Standards and Quality.* This document followed the Parker Morris approach in identifying the amount of space needed to allow rooms and dwellings to perform their allocated functions. Both the National Housing Federation's Guide to Standards and Quality and the Joseph Rowntree Foundation's Lifetime Homes standards set functionality requirements for rooms and dwellings rather than setting minimum floor areas.[58]

Space standards today

The United Kingdom has smaller space standards in comparison to those in Europe. The RIBA acknowledges in *Better Homes and Neighbourhoods* that the average floor space of a new dwelling in the United Kingdom is 76 square metres compared with 115 square metres in the Netherlands.[59] Furthermore, the report highlighted that the average new homes being sold today in England and Wales are smaller than those of 1920s.[60] However, in the report *High Density in Europe: Lessons for London* PRP Architects argue that it is wrong to assume that European and Dutch space standards are better than those in the United Kingdom.[61] The report states that many countries in Europe, including the Netherlands, also have poor quality housing with poor space standards.

In the report *Design and Quality Strategy,* published in April 2007, the Housing Corporation introduced recommendations for minimum standards for housing. This report aimed to deliver design quality through five key factors: (1) setting clear standards; (2) using the competitive framework to reward high standards; (3) quality design with agreed standards; (4) evaluating the impact on residents; and (5) supporting good practice.[62]

The Design Quality and Housing Quality Indicators

In 1999, the Design Quality Indicator (DQI) was developed to help all built environment stakeholders gain more value from the design of buildings and to assist in improving the quality of

↗ Donnybrook Quarter.

↘ The completed Summit House built at Allerton Bywater, Leeds.

buildings. The Design Quality Indicator bases its evaluation of design quality on the Vitruvian model of *firmitas* (build quality), *utilitas* (functionality) and *venustas* (impact). These three quality fields are separated into subsections with a detailed assessment of particular attributes. The DQI questionnaire is a short, non-technical set of questions that collect the views of different parties by looking at the functionality, build quality and impact of buildings. The DQI can be used by all stakeholders involved in the production of buildings.

The development of the DQI has been led by the Construction Industry Council with sponsorship from the DTI, CABE, Constructing Excellence and the Strategic Forum for Construction. The DQI questionnaire encompasses questions that are relevant at any stage of the development of a building and the tool can be revisited throughout the life of a project. There are four stages of the tool – brief, mid-design, ready for occupation and in-use.

Also in 1999, on behalf of the Department for the Transport, Local Government and the Regions (Now Department for Communities and Local Government) and the Housing Corporation, the architecture and design firm DEGW introduced the Housing Quality Indicator (HQI), providing a methodology for assessing the quality of new housing schemes. The system

allows an assessment of quality to be made on the basis of three main categories – location, design and performance, which break down further into ten 'quality indicators':

1. Location.
2. Site – visual impact, layout and landscaping.
3. Site – open space.
4. Site – routes and movement.
5. Unit – size.
6. Unit – layout.
7. Unit – noise, light and services.
8. Unit – accessibility.
9. Unit – energy, green and sustainability issues.
10. Performance in use.[63]

Design and access statements

In May 2006 the British government introduced changes to the planning application process. Circular 01/06, published in August 2006, gave guidance on changes to the development control system, making for the first time a formal requirement for design and access statements to accompany most types of planning applications.

A design and access statement is a document that explains the design thinking behind a planning application but is not part of the planning application. Statements usually include a written description, photographs, drawings and justification of the planning application.

The design and access statement are required to provide information covering the design process and physical characteristics of the scheme. The CABE publication *Design and Access Statements, How to Write and Read Them*, explains that the physical design characteristics of the scheme should be assessed by six factors: (1) use; (2) amount; (3) layout; (4) scale; (5) landscaping; and (6) appearance. The statement must also include two potential aspects of access, (1) vehicular and transport links; and (2) inclusive access.[64]

Low- and high-rise doll's houses and Dan Dare steel and glass towers? Design quality in the Thames Gateway

Context

Nothing but the best is acceptable to the Thames Gateway.[65]

The Thames Gateway is Britain's first 'eco-region' and currently the largest regeneration zone in Europe, with an area of 43 by 20 miles, covering both sides of the River Thames from the London Docklands to Southend and Sheerness. It contains some of the largest brownfield sites of London and includes areas of contaminated land from earlier industrial use, landfill sites, overhead electricity pylons and old gasworks.

In February 2003 the Office of the Deputy Prime Minister launched the Sustainable Communities Action Plan to construct 120,000 new dwellings by 2016 across the Thames Gateway, of which around 60,000 will be part of Greater London. This figure was revised in 2006 to 160,000 new dwellings; 25,000 new homes have been built in the Thames Gateway since 2003.

The British government's ambition to transform this region will be an important test of its commitment to delivering design quality. The implementation of this vision of design quality for the Thames Gateway is the responsibility of the Department for Communities and Local Government, English Partnerships, The Housing Corporation, regional development agencies and the Environment Agency. The statutory planning guidance is set by three regional planning bodies – the Greater London Authority, the South East of England Development Agency (SEEDA) and the East of England Development Agency (EEDA).

Early priority was to concentrate on urban areas with previous development. In 2007, the Department for Communities and Local Government set ten priority areas (see table opposite) for new housing and a new government department was created, the Homes and Communities Agency. The Agency intends to bring together the responsibility for land and finance to deliver new housing, community facilities and new infrastructure and will also work with local councils on the design and delivery of the new eco-towns. The agency will have operational responsibility for the delivery of the Thames Gateway.

Proposals for new housing in ten priority areas of the Thames Gateway, 2007

Location	Number of new housing units
Lower Lea Valley and Stratford	23,400
The Royals, including Canning Town	18,900
Greenwich Peninsula	13,200
Thurrock	12,200
Barking (Riverside and Town Centre)	10,500
Medway (Waterfront and Chattenden)	8,100
Basildon	6,700
Woolwich	6,100
Kent Thameside Waterfront	5,700
Ebbsfleet Valley	3,700

Source: Adapted from HM Government, Department for Communities and Local Government, Crown Copyright, *The Delivery Plan, The Thames Gateway* London: Department for Communities and Local Government, 2007, p. 44.

The government is supporting the development of greener homes through the Code for Sustainable Homes and a timetable for moving to zero-carbon building standards. Since 1 October 2007 HM Treasury regulations have set a stamp duty land tax exemption until 2012 for all new homes up to £500,000 that are built to a zero-carbon standard. Between 1 October 2007, when the policy came into force, and the end of November 2007, however, just three house buyers in the United Kingdom claimed stamp duty tax relief on the purchase of new zero-carbon homes.[66] If this low number of house buyers is to be believed, it indicates there may be a lack of demand for zero-carbon homes in the future and within the Thames Gateway.

The government will introduce a new eco quarter in the Gateway, similar to the planned eco-towns but within an existing urban area. The government has also announced it will spend £100 million on infrastructure in the Thames Gateway. The Department for Communities and Local Government states that quality in the Thames Gateway will only be established through clear aspirations:

The key to getting consistent better quality is being very clear about our collective expectation on standards for the Gateway and holding everyone who is part of the development process to account for meeting those standards.[67]

Controversies on the implementation of design quality in the Thames Gateway

The Department for Communities and Local Government has stated it is committed to provide better design quality in the Thames Gateway through a number of key initiatives:

- by ensuring the 'best of the best' housing developments are being built by introducing the Building for Life standard;

- through the Housing Corporation's initiative to develop quality and development standards for strategic sites;

- through John Egan's development of a comprehensive skills and training strategy to deliver sustainable communities;

- by increasing funding to the Commission for Architecture and the Built Environment for enabling and design review work;

- by establishing a Housing Quality Forum to disseminate best practice within the housing growth areas.[68]

The government also sees design quality being maintained through the appointment of the architect Terry Farrell as a design champion for the Thames Gateway Parklands. In *The Delivery Plan: The Thames Gateway*, the Department for Communities and Local Government establishes that design quality will be implemented by two further methods: by asking CABE to do a further Housing Audit in the Gateway in 2010 'to measure progress in improving design quality' and also by producing a 'design pact' for the Thames Gateway, demonstrating the commitment of the Department for Communities and Local Government, local agencies, local authorities and private developers to champion and implement good design across the Gateway.[69] This was launched at the Thames Gateway Forum in November 2007.

The Pact will highlight the role of design in shaping quality of life, stimulating economic development and encouraging innovation. The Building for Life Standard will be the measure of design quality...We intend to commission CABE to conduct a further housing audit in 2010 to measure progress.[70]

The Thames Gateway Design Pact has been described by CABE as a 'unifying commitment' to design quality in the

← Contemporary housing in Silvertown.

→ Abbotts Wharf.

↙ The Greenwich Millennium Village.

Gateway region. The design pact aims to 'help unlock the delivery of more homes'. It also aims to 'provide absolute clarity' about the actions needed to transform the quality of the Gateway over the next three years. [71] The pact establishes six principles necessary for successful quality:

1. Vision.
2. Leadership.
3. Well-networked places.
4. Adapting to climate change.
5. Cohesion and valuing places.
6. Design that includes.[72]

There has, however, been widespread criticism of newly constructed housing in the Thames Gateway. Some commentators have reported isolated communities in poor quality homes with few facilities and services. Lynsey Hanley, author of *Estates: An Intimate History* was dismayed when she visited Barking Reach, a new development on the Thames Gateway, comparing the newly constructed houses to those of shoeboxes.[73] In an article for *Building Design* the architect Eelco Hooftman argued that the new housing will consist of a number of shoddy sink estates with little imagination and vision:

> We are heading for a diaspora of speculative toy town sink estates, a potent mixture of low-rise and high tide. We have dull, shifty opportunism when what we need is a long-term vision where imagination can take hold.[74]

The Institute for Public Policy Research believes that the characterless and monotonous housing will result in home-owners not wanting to move to the Thames Gateway.[75] Peter Hall, Professor of Planning at University College London, one of the greatest critics of new housing on the Thames Gateway, states that the land along the Thames does not have adequate infrastructure for the construction of new housing and is prone to flooding. [76] The architect Richard Rogers is also critical of new housing that is being constructed on the Thames Gateway:

> Our most precious sites are being defined by alien lines of low- and high-rise doll's houses, occasionally interrupted by Dan Dare steel and glass towers with no regard for context or relationship with their surroundings. Tacky bungalows are creeping aimlessly along the banks of the Thames, one of the world's most magnificent rivers. Plastic clapboard and tiles, imitation stone, shoddy concrete and tiny windows facing the best views are symptoms of barbarity.[77]

Richard Rogers remains 'deeply concerned as to whether [the Thames Gateway] will fulfil its potential'.[78] He suggests that it is

One Gallions is a proposed new high density housing scheme on a site north-east of London City Airport and the Royal Docks within the Albert Basin Development Masterplan. The client's vision is to create a sustainable community development that will act as an exemplar scheme integrating the principles of sustainability, community, social inclusion, tolerance and economic vitality.

the government that is lacking vision and needs to employ architects in the decision-making process to make the scheme work. This, he believes, is because there is no proper policy framework for design excellence in the UK, stating:

> There are too many organisations, with too little focus on delivering quality. The government and its quangos and housebuilders need to put skilled architects at the forefront of the urban renaissance. Without them we shall never achieve our aspirations...Without a structural hierarchy, decision-making is left in a quagmire of mediocrity. Many of the delivery bodies operate first and foremost as land dealers and surveyors concerned with numbers and management, not design. Among the bodies I deal with, only the new London Thames Gateway has an architect on its board.[79]

However, Ian Abley, author of *Why is Construction so Backward?*, is firmly against the argument of putting architects into positions of power within the Thames Gateway. He does not believe that architects becoming more involved will benefit anyone other than those architects themselves. He states that since Labour came to power in 1997 they have appointed undemocratically elected representatives and quangos (for example, such as CABE) to positions of authority that have overruled those elected members and councillors, reducing the decision-making process. He believes this is not a recipe for quality in the built environment in the UK and could spell disaster in the Thames Gateway. As a result, Abley argues that government policy results in poor design quality as anyone who signs up for government programmes becomes a unelected arbiter of 'good design':

> The Sustainable Communities initiative is a further attack on professionalism, a restraint on the independence of planning officers, and an undemocratic weakening of the role of elected planning committee members. The inertia of Design Quality Indicators, focus groups and wider consultation will set in, with CABE as 'English Futures' always in evidence as the unelected arbiter of 'good design'. 'Good' architects will be those unquestioning types who have learned to speak 'sustainababble' and 'communitwaddle' at CABE reviews and at John Egan's academy. Consensus and collaboration kill creativity.[80]

Ian Abley goes on to suggest that what is needed is a stronger and more centralised leadership in the Thames Gateway, for example from the Greater London Authority. The establishment of the new Homes and Communities Agency will create a more centralised authority of new housing in the Thames Gateway. How, therefore, will this new agency evaluate and assess design quality to help deliver the 160,000 new homes that are planned in the Thames Gateway? The Department for Communities and Local Government has stated that it intends to conduct a further housing audit for the Gateway in 2010. It is proposed that in this audit no housing scheme will be assessed as 'poor', and at least 50 per cent of new housing schemes will be 'good' or 'very good'. By 2015, 100 per cent of housing developments, it is proposed, will be assessed as 'good' or 'very good'.[81]

It can be argued, however, that both the Housing Audit and the Building for Life Standard are not enforcing and monitoring design quality sufficiently enough within new housing developments in the Thames Gateway and in the United Kingdom. Assessing completed housing projects as 'poor', 'average', 'good' or 'very good' from a set of defined criteria does not provide a sufficiently high incentive to deliver quality for the average new housing development. Both the Calcutt Review[82] and the Home Builders Federation[83] recognise that the CABE Housing Audit and Building for Life Standard are voluntary assessments and developers do not have to apply the schemes. Furthermore, the Calcutt Review states that the CABE and Building for Life Standard assessment criteria are controversial and are not accepted by the whole housebuilding industry, as the standards do not cover all aspects of design quality. The Home Builders Federation also states that the CABE assessment needs to be treated with considerable caution due to the unbalanced approach of the assessment criteria.

The Calcutt Review[84] suggests, instead, that design quality should be measured by customer satisfaction and not by a subjective set of criteria. It recommends that a new assessment should be developed with the Building for Life Standard as a starting point but extended for both larger housing developments and for individual houses. The Calcutt Review also recommends that CABE should reconsider the housebuilding design review process and that, if a scheme has passed an assessment process, it should not be subject to any further objections or conditions in relation to design quality imposed by planning authorities. The Campaign to Protect Rural England also recommended that

the government extend the Building for Life Standard by pursuing a design 'quality threshold' for the Thames Gateway, which takes into consideration local context and standards of construction, attractiveness of design and layout, access to amenities, incorporation of green open space and the impact of electricity distribution systems.[85]

The Calcutt Review and the Campaign to Protect Rural England both make valid contributions to the housing debate in the Thames Gateway. In practice, a design quality threshold, which further maintains and ensures that quality is provided, could be incorporated into an extended design and access statement just for the region surrounding the Thames Gateway.

In the Netherlands, design quality within new housing developments is not measured by the same set of criteria as in the United Kingdom, but instead by resident surveys. It is common practice for local councils to publish satisfaction ratings of housing residents. In Vathorst, for example, a yearly report of housing statistics is published by the City Council of Amersfoort.[86] This report contains surveys of every new housing development in the surrounding municipality. Tables are provided of the level of satisfaction in the neighbourhood, levels of social cohesion,[87] satisfaction with regard to the greenery nearby and how people appreciate the design of their house. Vathorst boasts a higher standard than the average housing development in Amersfoort in almost all categories.

There are therefore a number of important challenges in the Thames Gateway. In the creation of the Design Pact and the Homes and Communities Agency the government will need to ensure there is a high level of coordination that promotes high-quality standards for new housing in the Gateway. The government itself admits that high quality has not yet been achieved in the Gateway and quality needs to be tackled. 'We are not yet at the point where everyone, including Gateway residents, can be confident that every housing development will be high quality.'[88]

Accordia, Cambridge

Context

Accordia is a good example of high-quality new housing in the United Kingdom. The project received strong support from CABE and the local planning authority and won the 2006 Housing Design Award. The development consists of 212 houses and 166 apartments. Thirty per cent of the dwellings were constructed as affordable homes. The design brief asked for an exceptional urban environment with a combination of space, landscaping and good environmental performance. From the outset Cambridge City Council established a leading role in the design of the development, by stating that it would only grant planning permission to Countryside Properties if it were to achieve an exemplary standard of quality.

The development is located on a 9.5 hectare site, 1.3 miles outside the centre of Cambridge on brownfield land that was formerly occupied by low-rise government offices. There is a well-considered variety of housing within the scheme, with 26 different housing types and 48 different apartment types. Density is also mixed, up to 65 dwellings per hectare. The dwellings range from one-bedroom affordable apartments of 45 square metres to apartments with several bedrooms of up to 145 square metres, from medium-sized houses of 90 square metres with mews apartments to luxurious five-bedroom courtyard villas of 350 square metres. The architect and masterplanner, Feilden Clegg Bradley, designed 230 dwellings (65 per cent of the dwellings) and introduced two additional architectural practices to the project to achieve a variety of design across the site. Maccreanor Lavington designed 113 dwellings (25 per cent), including the row houses and apartments, and Alison Brooks designed 35 dwellings (10 per cent), consisting of several blocks of flats and four houses. The three architecture firms worked within a

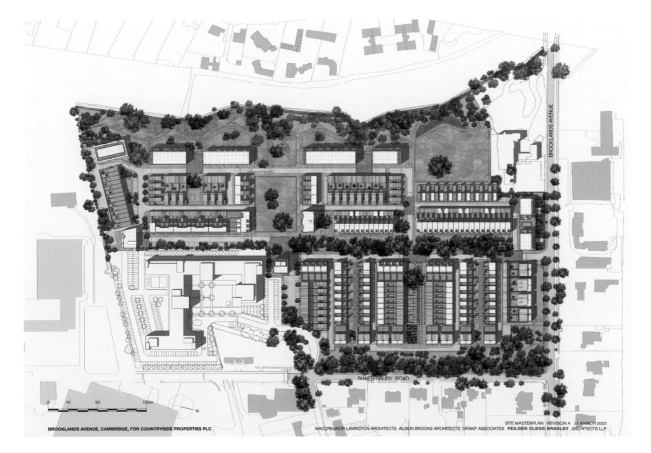

BROOKLANDS AVENUE, CAMBRIDGE, FOR COUNTRYSIDE PROPERTIES PLC   MACCREANOR LAVINGTON ARCHITECTS ALISON BROOKS ARCHITECTS GRANT ASSOCIATES **FEILDEN CLEGG BRADLEY** ARCHITECTS LLP

↑   Site masterplan of Accordia.

←   A semi-detached house at Accordia by Alison Brooks Architects.

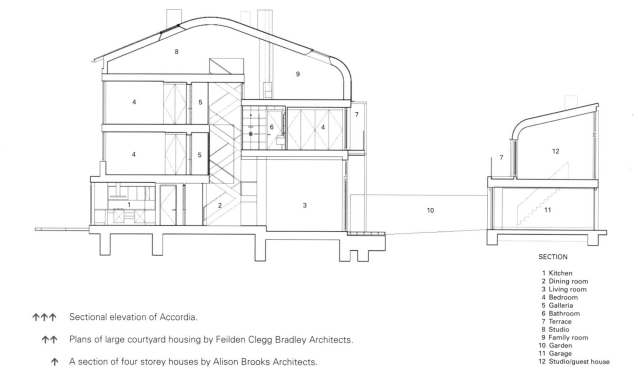

↑↑↑　Sectional elevation of Accordia.

↑↑　Plans of large courtyard housing by Feilden Clegg Bradley Architects.

↑　A section of four storey houses by Alison Brooks Architects.

SECTION

1 Kitchen
2 Dining room
3 Living room
4 Bedroom
5 Galleria
6 Bathroom
7 Terrace
8 Studio
9 Family room
10 Garden
11 Garage
12 Studio/guest house

Character

tightly defined palette of materials implementing a number of constraints, such as the type of external materials, with brick, timber and aluminium composite frames, copper roofing and cladding.

The landscaping spaces and internal courtyards give a distinctive identity and a contemporary feel. There are over 700 mature trees on the site and a number of private and public spaces. The layout of the masterplan is coherent and well structured.

↑   A new housing block at Accordia.

Roads, parking
and pedestrianisation

The masterplan included a balance of landscaped pedestrian lanes, mews streets with shared communal spaces, car parking and public bicycle stands, as well as integrated secure cycle parking for all dwellings. Vehicular access is via a T-junction off the main road, Brooklands Avenue, creating a large cul-de-sac.

The larger town houses were designed on narrow roads to limit car use. There are a number of footpaths in and around the site and a new cycling route has been built. Most car parking is provided on the street; however, 30 per cent of the dwellings have garages. The larger apartment blocks have underground garages and the largest houses have a double car garage.

Design and construction

The architects have used the courtyards and buildings of Cambridge colleges and Georgian houses as a design precedent. The walls have been constructed with distinctive yellow bricks, high ceilings, and rows of chimneys. Each house has a relatively narrow plot, with a 5.2 metres plot width and up to 3 metres floor to ceiling heights. Dwellings have windows that open onto quieter private open spaces. There is a good attention to detail and a composition of materials and forms.

The larger-scale apartment buildings and terraces are associated with the larger open spaces and are typically on an east/west orientation to minimise the overshadowing of the smaller adjacent homes. Lower terraces and courts have been planned around more intimate landscape spaces with terraced gardens. On the main road, Brooklands Avenue, the houses are three to four storeys high and bordered by landscaping with protruding balconies.

↑   Rear terraced housing overlooking a shared green space.

↖   Two storey houses with private garages.

←   Different approaches to articulation of the façade of three storey houses overlooking the street.

↗   A good environmental performance was achieved at Accordia for each dwelling type in water usage, the materials used and methods used for construction.

↗↗   Homes have been planned to be adaptable so that they can accommodate the changing needs of the residents and respond to changing technologies.

Environment and community

Sustainable design was considered an important part of the design of Accordia. A good environmental performance was achieved for each dwelling type in water usage, the materials used and methods used for construction. The materials used are a Cambridge stock brick for the external façades of the houses and copper and green oak for the apartments. Much of the construction was fabricated off-site to increase speed of construction, reduce waste and to improve site safety and environmental performance.

Feilden Clegg Bradley described the design of the scheme as 'urban rugs on a carpet of landscape', with landscaped gardens that took their inspiration from the college courtyards of Cambridge. Drainage measures involving permeable surfaces, green roofs and reed beds help retain rainwater on site to sustain the extensive landscape resource. Homes have been planned to be adaptable so that they can accommodate the changing needs of the residents and respond to changing technologies; house-buyers have the possibility to buy solar or photovoltaic panels and add them at a later date. The excellent use of detail and insulation means performance is good. The scheme outperforms building regulations with good standards of airtightness.

Accordia, Cambridge

General

Site area 9.5 hectare site	**Density** 40 dph overall with landscaping (65dph if gardens excluded)
Total number of inhabitants/dwellings 378 dwellings. (212 houses and 166 apartments) 130 people in 40 units	**Housing mix by tenure** 30% affordable housing, 70% private housing (76% for rent and 24% shared ownership)
Average number of people per dwelling 2	**Percentage of commercial use** Approximately 5% (119 m² workspace)

Character

	Objectives	Strengths	Weaknesses	Evaluation	Design quality standard
1.	Does the scheme feel like a place with a distinctive character?	Contemporary and thoughtful housing, generating character.	—	Distinctive character. The landscaping spaces and internal courtyards give a distinctive identity and a contemporary feel.	Very good
2.	Do buildings exhibit architectural quality?	Good architectural design with good features.	—	Very good architectural quality.	Very good
3.	Are streets defined by a coherent and well-structured layout?	One main junction off Brooklands Road with adjacent roads leading off main entrance road.	Narrow roads difficult to drive through but has been designed to limit car use.	—	Good
4.	Do buildings and layout make it easy to find your way around?	—	—	Easy to find one's way around. Good road layout.	Good
5.	Does the scheme exploit existing buildings, landscape or topography?	Good use of existing site and topography.	—	The site was brownfield land that was formerly occupied by low-rise government offices.	Good

Roads, parking and pedestrianization

	Objectives	Strengths	Weaknesses	Evaluation	Design quality standard
6.	Does the building layout take priority over the roads and car parking, so that highways do not dominate?	Good balance between the road and public, semi-public and private spaces.	—	—	Good
7.	Are the streets pedestrian, cycle and vehicle friendly?	Most car parking is provided on the street; however, 30 per cent of the dwellings have garages.	—	Pedestrian streets, mews streets with shared areas, and integrated cycle parking for all dwellings.	Good
8.	Is car parking well-integrated so it supports the street scene?	Discreet car parking. Good variety of car parking. Most car parking is provided on the street; however, 30 per cent of the dwellings have garages. The larger apartment blocks have underground garages and the largest houses have a double car garage.	—	Car parking ratio is 1.26:1. The larger apartment blocks have underground garages and the largest houses have a double car garage.	Good
9.	Does the scheme integrate with existing roads, paths and surrounding development?	—	—	Good balance between the road and public, semi-public and private spaces and surrounding development.	Good
10.	Are public spaces and pedestrian routes overlooked and do they feel safe?	—	—	All streets and public spaces overlooked and feels safe.	Good

Design and construction

	Objectives	Strengths	Weaknesses	Evaluation	Design quality standard
11.	Is the design specific to the scheme?	The design is specific to the scheme.	—	Very distinct and characteristic design.	Very good
12.	Is public space well-designed and does it have suitable management arrangements in place?	—	Little in the way of public space.	A few semi-public spaces but little in the way of public space.	Average
13.	Do buildings or spaces outperform statutory minima, such as building regulations?	—	—	Exceeds building regulations.	Good
14.	Has the scheme made use of advances in construction or technology that enhance its performance, quality and attractiveness?	A good environmental performance was achieved for each dwelling type in water usage, the materials used and methods used for construction.	—	Much of the construction was fabricated off-site to increase speed of construction, reduce waste and to improve site safety and environmental performance.	Good
15.	Do internal spaces and a layout allow for adaption, conversion or extension?	—	—	Some flats and houses can be adapted internally.	Average

Environment and community

	Objectives	Strengths	Weaknesses	Evaluation	Design quality standard
16.	Does the development have easy access to public transport?	—	—	Good bus links into Cambridge.	Average
17.	Does the development have any features that reduce its environmental impact?	The materials used are a Cambridge stock brick for the external façades of the houses and copper and Green green Oak oak for the apartments.	—	A good environmental performance was achieved for each dwelling type in water usage, the materials used and methods used for construction.	Good
18.	Is there a tenure mix that reflects the needs of the local community?	The dwellings range from one-bedroom affordable apartments of 45 square metres to apartments with several bedrooms of up to 145 square metres, from medium sized houses of 90 square metres with mews apartments to luxurious five bedroom courtyard villas of 350 square metres.	—	Well considered variety of housing.	Good
19.	Is there a mix of accommodation that reflects the needs and aspirations of the local community?	—	—	Good mixture of blocks of flats and row houses.	Good
20.	Does the development provide community facilities, such as a school, park play areas, shops, pubs or cafes?	—	—	Good play areas and landscaped spaces but a lack of community facilities.	Average

The Greenwich Millennium Village

Context

The Greenwich Millennium Village was established as part of the Millennium Communities programme in 1997 by English Partnerships, with guidance from the Urban Task Force and the Millennium Villages Advisory Panel. The programme was intended to set a standard for twenty-first century living and serve as a model for the creation of new communities. The Deputy Prime Minister John Prescott promised a new community that would set a benchmark for new housing and an exemplar of sustainable development with high energy efficient and adaptable housing. The Office of the Deputy Prime Minister, now the Department for Communities and Local Government, sought to set high standards of design by minimising resource consumption, and maximising environmental capital, social inclusion, community participation and commercial viability.[89] The Greenwich Millennium Village was the first millennium project and won a Building for Life Gold award for commitment to design standards.

The Greenwich Millennium Village Limited led the consortium, in a partnership with Countryside Properties, Taylor Woodrow and English Partnerships. The masterplanners were Erskine Tovatt Architects and the design architects for phase one and phase two for the housing were Proctor Matthews. The development was designed to provide high-density innovative housing that would provide 20 per cent affordable housing in a mixed-use development and with good public transport links.

This is to be done through encouraging innovation in building technologies, increasing economic and social self-sufficiency, achieving exemplar standards of functional urban design and focusing on sustainable development that addresses energy and conservation issues and building technologies.[90]

There were a number of established targets in the Village and quality reviews were established throughout the design and construction. These targets included reducing construction waste, the reduction of embodied energy and water consumption. To date, 1,095 new dwellings have been constructed and future development between 2007 and 2014 will increase this number to a total of 2,750 dwellings. English Partnerships has set additional standards in the future construction phase, which

include improving noise insulation by 10 per cent above building regulations Part E (2004) and achieving as a minimum the Silver Standard in the Building for Life Standard accreditation.

The Greenwich Millennium Village has received mixed reviews from its residents. Chris Homes points out in *A New Vision for Housing* that resident surveys have shown high levels of satisfaction, especially regarding the friendliness of the community and appreciation of the location next to the river.[91] However, on Channel 4's Dispatches programme *Britain's Bad Housing* other residents complained of the poor quality inside

↗ The design of the Greenwich Millennium Village has sought to maximise shared and private spaces with landscaping.

← A variety of colours, forms and materials of new housing at the Greenwich Millennium Village.

↙   New public space surrounded by contrasted stepped roofline at Holly Court.

↓   This interesting façade has been designed with projecting balconies, large windows and solar shading.

→   An internal street at the centre of the development.

↘   A detail of two adjoining properties illustrating the attention paid to colour, materiality and projection.

the homes with bad workmanship, poor finishing and poor acoustic insulation between walls and floors.[92] The architect Graham Towers in *An Introduction to Urban Design: At Home in the City* also criticised the scheme:

> Most disappointingly, and despite some good quality high-density housing designed by Erskine himself, the urban design quality of the new village is poor. There is a lack of space formation and enclosure and far too much open space. The whole scheme is far too open, much too dominated by vehicles to make it a model for the new urbanity.[93]

The millennium scheme has been reported to cost more to construct than planned, to match the aspiration of high standards. As a result, dwellings have sold for higher prices. The profit or surplus per housing unit was the same as a conventional scheme but profit as a percentage of finished value of the scheme is lower, 16.5 per cent compared with 20 per cent of conventional schemes.[94]

Character

The design is characterised by a variety of roof types with a use of warm colours. The design is visually bold, with a mix of balconies, brickwork, timber cladding and metal cladding. Some apartments have good views over the River Thames whilst other apartments overlook the internal courtyard.

Roads, parking and pedestrianisation

The design sought to reduce the use of the car and to create many public areas for the pedestrian. The majority of car parking, as a result, has been located below ground or in two-storey

car parks at the perimeter of the development. There is one main vehicular road around Maurer Court that is lined with trees and contains some on-street car parking. There is a two-storey underground car park directly beneath Maurer Court containing 292 parking spaces. Bicycle storage has been located within secure bike stations and there is a shared cycle path adjacent to the pedestrian footpath. Pedestrian routes are well overlooked and the pedestrian public courtyards feel safe.

Design and construction

Maurer Court was constructed in the third phase of housing development built at Greenwich Millennium Village. It was funded by English Partnerships and opened in 2001. Maurer Court sits on the north-east corner of the site between the River Thames and the ecology park. It has been designed to act as a landmark, with barrel vaulted roofs and colourful panels. The barrel vaulted roofs give a distinctive identity and a playful design style for the development. Maurer Court comprises of three buildings and contains a gated courtyard garden. It is constructed alongside new commercial and retail development, a new school and new healthcare facilities.

The structure of the dwellings is in-situ reinforced concrete frame construction. There are metal infill cladding panels with render, timber, banded decorative brickwork and stack bonded blockwork. Stud partition walls separate rooms within flats, following the idea that residents can adapt their flats. The design sought to maximise solar gain, natural light and ventilation. Off-site manufacture and component assembly was used for bathroom units, which were delivered as complete rooms to the main block of the 177 flats. Cladding and roof panels were factory made and the plant was delivered in component parts.

The typical unit areas are 52 square metres for a one-bedroom flat and 90 square metres for a two-bedroom flat. The brief required that 25 per cent of the land and 20 per cent of the housing units be allocated to affordable housing and that the proposals meet high standards of construction, landscape and urban design.

Environment and community

The design of the Greenwich Millennium Village had very specific environmental and quality standards that developers were required to meet. As a result, this was the first development in the United Kingdom to achieve the Building Research Establishment's EcoHome 'Excellent' rating. A key factor in the high sustainable targets was the implementation of a combined heat and power facility. This was a fully managed service, which meant that residents did not need to individually maintain boilers and is estimated to have provided 65 per cent reduction of carbon dioxide emissions for the development.[95]

There are good transport links. Six bus routes operate in and around the development and there is a bus route to the underground station at North Greenwich. The residents have been active in creating a community, setting up a residents association and creating a resident-owned company that is responsible for providing management services.

↑   This front façade combines a combination of solar shading, projected balconies and a variety of materials.

↖   Bright and distinctive colours give life and character to the development.

←   A street designed for the pedestrian.

The Greenwich Millennium Village

General

Site area	**Density**
72 acres in total	Approximately 200 dwellings per hectare
Total number of inhabitants/dwellings	**Housing mix by tenure**
2,750 dwellings in total by 2014	Earlier developments contain 20% social housing, 80% private housing. The newer developments contain 35% affordable units and 30/70 tenure split socially rented and private.
Average number of people per dwelling	**Percentage of commercial use**
2	10% (4,500m² of commercial space in total)

Character

	Objectives	Strengths	Weaknesses	Evaluation	Design quality standard
1.	Does the scheme feel like a place with a distinctive character?	The barrel vaulted roofs give a distinctive identity and a playful design.	—	There are a variety of roof types, façades, solar shading and materials with the use of warm colours.	Good
2.	Do buildings exhibit architectural quality?	The design is visually bold with a mix of balconies, brickwork, timber cladding and metal cladding.	There have been reports of poor workmanship, and poor acoustic insulation in internal walls between flats.	Good architectural quality overall. Some reports of poor acoustic insulation of walls and poor workmanship.	Good
3.	Are streets defined by a coherent and well-structured layout?	Coherent and simple planning of streets. Good access to the Thames and The O₂.	—	There is one main vehicular road around Maurer Court which is lined with trees and contains some on-street car parking.	Good
4.	Do buildings and layout make it easy to find your way around?	—	—	Easy to get around with one main access road in and out of the development.	Good
5.	Does the scheme exploit existing buildings, landscape or topography?	Good views over the Thames and into the surrounding parks and green spaces.	—	Some apartments have good views over the river Thames whilst other apartments overlook the internal courtyards and park. The overall site orientation of the buildings have been designed to maximise solar gain.	Good

Roads, parking and pedestrianization

6.	Does the building layout take priority over the roads and car parking, so that highways do not dominate?	Highways do not dominate but provide easy and effective links around the development.	It has been designed to be virtually car free; however, many cars still use the site and parking for visitors is a problem.	The design sought to reduce the use of the car and to create many public areas for the pedestrian.	Good
7.	Are the streets pedestrian, cycle and vehicle friendly?	There are many pedestrian and cycle paths which have been well planned.	—	Bicycle storage has been located within secure bike stations and there is a shared cycle path adjacent to the pedestrian footpath.	Good
8.	Is car parking well-integrated so it supports the street scene?	There is a two-storey underground car park directly beneath Maurer Court containing 292 parking spaces.	Parking for visitors is a problem and there are not enough on-street spaces.	The majority of car parking has been located below ground or in two storey car parks at the perimeter of the development.	Average
9.	Does the scheme integrate with existing roads, paths and surrounding development?	Good connections to the Thames, The O₂ and the main roundabout.	—	The one main access road integrates well with the existing main roundabout and road.	Average
10.	Are public spaces and pedestrian routes overlooked and do they feel safe?	Pedestrian routes are well overlooked and the pedestrian public courtyards feel safe.	—	Pedestrian routes are well overlooked and the pedestrian public courtyards feel safe.	Good

Design and construction

	Objectives	Strengths	Weaknesses	Evaluation	Design quality standard
11.	Is the design specific to the scheme?	It has been designed to act as a landmark with barrel vaulted roofs and colourful panels.	—	High-density innovative housing which is specific to the scheme. Good variety of design.	Good
12.	Is public space well-designed and does it have suitable management arrangements in place?	Greenwich Millennium Village Limited was established for the responsibility of the long-term management of the Village. The company is owned by the residents and owners.	—	An active residents' association that deals with management arrangements has been established.	Good
13.	Do buildings or spaces outperform statutory minima, such as building regulations?	Out-performs environmental criteria and targets.	—	Water efficient appliances. Grey water recycling. Recycling bins in kitchens. Flexible 'lifetime' homes.	Good
14.	Has the scheme made use of advances in construction or technology that enhance its performance, quality and attractiveness?	Cladding and roof panels were factory made and the plant was delivered in component parts.	—	Off-site manufacture and component assembly was used for bathroom units which were delivered as complete rooms to the main block of the 177 flats.	Good
15.	Do internal spaces and a layout allow for adaption, conversion or extension?	Greater levels of adaptability were designed by using pre-engineered steel framed structures with standardised connections.	Many internal walls have poor acoustic insulation.	Stud partition walls separate rooms within flats following the idea that residents can adapt their flats.	Average

Environment and community

	Objectives	Strengths	Weaknesses	Evaluation	Design quality standard
16.	Does the development have easy access to public transport?	Public transport links have been improved and the site is close to North Greenwich underground station.	—	There are good transport links. Six bus routes operate in and around the development and there is a bus route to the underground station at North Greenwich.	Good
17.	Does the development have any features that reduce its environmental impact?	Achieves the EcoHome 'Excellent' rating. The new Ecology Park covers 50 acres contains many new trees, shrubs and a new lake.	—	Planning conditions included a target of 80% reduction in embodied energy, 50% reduction in construction waste and 25% reduction in car usage within 10 years. Water efficient appliances. Grey water recycling. Recycling bins in kitchens.	Very good
18.	Is there a tenure mix that reflects the needs of the local community?	Earlier developments contain 20% social housing, 80% private housing. The newer developments contain 35% affordable units and 30/70 tenure split socially rented and private.	—	Provides 20 per cent affordable housing in a mixed used development.	Good
19.	Is there a mix of accommodation that reflects the needs and aspirations of the local community?	There is a good mix of accommodation.	Lack of shopping facilities.	There is a lack of shopping facilities but a good mix of accommodation.	Good
20.	Does the development provide community facilities, such as a school, park play areas, shops, pubs or cafes?	There are several categories of play areas with informal areas, a variety of types of recreation and community and school facilities.	Lack of shopping facilities.	Received mixed reviews from its residents. The new Ecology Park covers 50 acres contains many new trees, shrubs and a new lake.	Good

The Staiths, Gateshead

Context

The Staiths is an 800-dwelling development on the banks of the River Tyne in Gateshead. It was designed in collaboration with George Wimpey, Wayne and Geraldine Hemingway, Ian Derby Partnership and Gateshead Council. The site had previously housed the Redheugh gas works and was unused since the 1990 Gateshead International Garden Festival. The Staiths was awarded third place out of 93 schemes in the 2005 CABE commission Housing Audit assessing the design quality of new homes in the North East, North West and Yorkshire and Humber. The development is a model of good quality new housing and an example of a successful collaboration between large housebuilder, designer, architect and local council.

The design brief proposed a forward-thinking design for a vibrant community. The defining concept was choice; allowing people to choose their elevation, layout and housing type, and offering residents influence and control over where they lived. The former Red or Dead founder Wayne Hemingway, a designer and town planner, criticised Britain's new housing in an article for the *Independent* newspaper, in what he called the 'Wimpeyfication' and 'Barrattification' of bland and monotonous new housing that he witnessed being constructed.[96] Hemingway's comments led to the housebuilder Wimpey commissioning Hemingway and his wife to deliver a new housing development to demonstrate they could design a good quality new housing development at an affordable price.

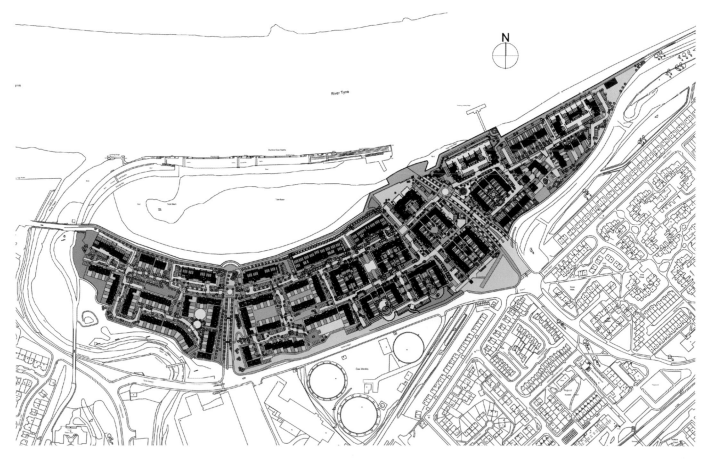

↑   Masterplan of the Staiths.

←   A shared community courtyard at the Staiths

113

The scheme has good bus links, and transport connections have been well located so that all residents can reach a bus stop within 400 metres. There is one car parking space per home. The Staiths has implemented the philosophy of the Home Zone with the support from Gateshead Council and by a £400,000 grant from the Department for Transport. The Home Zone Challenge Fund was established in the United Kingdom in 2001 to create a more harmonious relationship between pedestrians and vehicles. It is an experimental scheme introducing speed limits in new housing areas and was influenced from European models including the Dutch equivalent of Home Zone, named *woonerf,* and was also encouraged by the Task Force report *Towards an Urban Renaissance.* As a result, speed limits have been set to 10 mph and streets have been graded into more defined wider and narrower roads. The entrance road into the Staiths is a wide two-lane avenue with cars and pedestrians separated by defined roads and pavements. As the car travels through the site, the roads become narrower and pavements become wider.

There are a number of pedestrian areas, children's playgrounds and communal areas in the Staiths. Most housing has south facing communal gardens named by the designers as 'pocket parks' with facilities for all age groups, from innovative play areas to shared gas barbecues.

Character

The Staiths has a well-defined character. There are a variety of housing types with different kinds of roofs, consisting of two-storey houses, three-storey townhouses and a mix of apartments and flats. Two prominent high-density apartment blocks overlook the River Tyne. There is a sense of individuality, as each dwelling uses a different range of colours and a variety of materials including brickwork, cedar wood cladding and six types of timber front doors.

Design and construction

There are three terraced U-shaped housing blocks with a large mix of dwelling types with public and semi-public external spaces. There is a wide range of internal and external variations and dwellings have been constructed in brick and block with render and cedar cladding. Dwelling sizes range from 46.9 square metres to 130 square metres.

←   A variety of forms and materials at the Staiths.

↙   The varied roofline of a new housing terrace.

↓   View from above of the arrangement of a typical housing block.

Environment and community

The nature of the brownfield site made it possible to reuse some existing infrastructure such as access roads. Most new construction materials and elements were sourced locally. Site conditions on the former gasworks meant that a sustainable drainage system could not be considered. Cycling is encouraged by providing cycle parking. Each house has a cycle space and there are communal cycle sheds. All residents were given £50 contribution towards the purchase of a bicycle. Any remaining trees on the site were retained. There are a number of communal areas with well-planned children's play areas, for which each phase of the project has its own play strategy. There are timber enclosures with barbeques and eating areas.

←   Rear private garden of a terraced house leads to a shared communal courtyard.

↑   The elevation of varying roof forms overlooking the central access road.

↗   The rear courtyards have shared seating and a communal barbeque.

The Staiths, Gateshead

General

Site area	**Density**
40 acre brownfield site	58 per hectare
Total number of inhabitants/dwellings	**Housing mix by tenure**
Over 800 dwellings with 2000 inhabitants	Six basic types with 33 variations (typical unit area 46.9m2 to 130m^2).
(158 dwellings constructed so far)	100% private housing with no social housing
Average number of people per dwelling	**Percentage of commercial use**
2/3	1% (3 retail units)

Character

	Objectives	Strengths	Weaknesses	Evaluation	Design quality standard
1.	Does the scheme feel like a place with a distinctive character?	Good contemporary individual character with a mix of heights and different type of dwellings.	The taller apartment building next to the river not as distinctive in character as the houses.	Good design of varying typologies give the scheme a distinctive character. The existing grade II listed pier gives the river character.	Very good
2.	Do buildings exhibit architectural quality?	Good architectural design with a wide range of colours, typologies, materials and layouts.	—	—	Good
3.	Are streets defined by a coherent and well-structured layout?	—	—	Good well-planned central access road leading to surrounding quieter roads.	Good
4.	Do buildings and layout make it easy to find your way around?	—	—	The larger apartment dwellings by the river make way finding straightforward.	Good
5.	Does the scheme exploit existing buildings, landscape or topography?	Good design of private gardens onto south facing gardens.	—	No sign of existing gas works which previously existed on the site. The existing grade II listed pier gives the river character.	Good

Roads, parking and pedestrianization

6.	Does the building layout take priority over the roads and car parking, so that highways do not dominate?	Good design of soft landscaping so roads and parking do not dominate.	—	The emphasis on people and communal areas make the building layout and public areas take priority.	Good
7.	Are the streets pedestrian, cycle and vehicle friendly?	Good attention to cycle lanes and cycle stores in communal areas.	—	Well-located housing scheme next to the cycle network and good use of cycle stores.	Very good
8.	Is car parking well-integrated so it supports the street scene?	Parking well-integrated. One parking space per household.	—	Lack of garages in scheme gives greater character to relationship between housing and street.	Good
9.	Does the scheme integrate with existing roads, paths and surrounding development?	—	—	Well-sited scheme on former gas works and next to river and well-linked to existing roads.	Good
10.	Are public spaces and pedestrian routes overlooked and do they feel safe?	Well-designed public spaces give a communal feel to the scheme.	The signs demonstrated that the public spaces can be noisy.	The scheme feels safe and all public spaces and routes are overlooked.	Good

Design and construction

	Objectives	Strengths	Weaknesses	Evaluation	Design quality standard
11.	Is the design specific to the scheme?	Well-considered and designed scheme; can be a model for future developments.	—	The design is specific to the scheme but can be replicated anywhere.	Very good
12.	Is public space well-designed and does it have suitable management arrangements in place?	Excellent communal areas giving life to scheme with well-planned children's play areas.	The public spaces can be noisy.	Local authority managed rubbish collection and recycling. The aim in the future is to allow residents to control and manage their own management arrangements.	Very good
13.	Do buildings or spaces outperform statutory minima, such as building regulations?	Complies with building regulations standards.	—	Buildings do not outperform building regulations but do comply with building regulations standards.	Average
14.	Has the scheme made use of advances in construction or technology that enhance its performance, quality and attractiveness?	Advances with the design of roof trusses. Lots of soft landscaping, new-planted trees, more than other housing schemes.	Reports from some residents of poor workmanship but difficult to see from the street.	Standard construction techniques with good variety and use of materials.	Average
15.	Do internal spaces and a layout allow for adaption, conversion or extension?	Many spaces are open plan so can be converted easily.	Little in the way of indoor storage, small bedrooms and difficult to extend for new conversions.	Small bedrooms and internal spaces; however, spaces can be converted as they are open plan.	Average

Environment and community

	Objectives	Strengths	Weaknesses	Evaluation	Design quality standard
16.	Does the development have easy access to public transport?	All residents are within 400 metres of a bus stop with only a short ride into the centre of Newcastle.	—	Well-considered design to local transport networks. No river network as yet.	Good
17.	Does the development have any features that reduce its environmental impact?	Lots of soft landscaping, new-planted trees, more than other housing schemes.	The design could have pushed for more sustainable materials and features.	Good design of communal bins and recycling. Good use of landscaping with many new trees.	Good
18.	Is there a tenure mix that reflects the needs of the local community?	Good mix of housing that reflects the needs of the new residents.	—		Very good
19.	Is there a mix of accommodation that reflects the needs and aspirations of the local community?	Good mix of housing that reflects the needs of the new residents.	—	Very well designed mix of accommodation enhancing the vitality of the community.	Very good
20.	Does the development provide community facilities, such as a school, park play areas, shops, pubs or cafes?	Three retail units provided when the sales centre is converted.	There could have been more retail units; however, the communal areas make up for the lack of community facilities.	Good design of communal areas.	Average

Donnybrook Quarter, London

Context

Donnybrook Quarter is a low-rise, high-density new housing development on a busy corner site in East London. Peter Barber Architects were commissioned by the Circle 33 Housing Trust in 2003, after they were selected as a winner of the Architecture Foundations' 'Innovations in Housing' competition. It has since won a Housing Design Award and the Royal Academy Architecture Prize and can be seen as a model of new urban housing that has benefited from new planning and housing policies. The policies can be traced back to Lord Rogers' Urban Task Force from 1997, which gave a number of recommendations for new housing, including implementing a new zoning policy. Recommendations also included better connections to public transport, green spaces that are well integrated into the urban realm creating distinctive characters, and the introduction of new planning guidelines that allowed the construction of higher density urban housing between 30 to 50 dwellings per hectare,

Donnybrook is easily accessible and well connected to public transport and community facilities and services. The aim of the design was that space is used efficiently, is safe, accessible and user-friendly. Donnybrook offers a high-quality public realm with a large tree-lined public area within the centre of the scheme, and is pedestrian, cycle and vehicle friendly. It is close to Victoria Park and has a number of private patio spaces and balconies. It is generally well-integrated with the neighbouring buildings and the local area, in terms of scale, density, layout and access. The scheme density is around 400 habitable rooms per hectare.

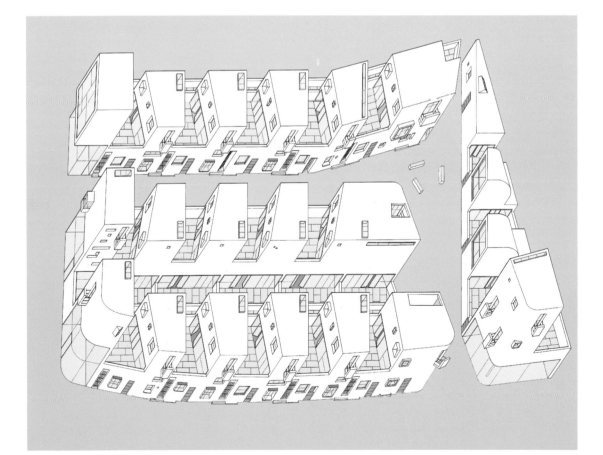

↗   Axonometric drawing of Donnybrook Quarter.

←   View of Donnybrook from the access road.

Character

The scheme is laid out around the two streets of Old Ford Road and Parnell Road. The new residential terrace follows the curve of Parnell Road along the eastern edge of the site. At its north end the terrace rises to a maximum of four storeys, marking an entrance to the development.

The design was specific to the scheme, but a later version of the same design has been constructed in Tanner Street in the Thames Gateway, also by Peter Barber Architects. Front doorways have been designed so that residents can create a sense of ownership and the opportunity for personalisation by adding their own plant pots and hanging baskets. The white rendered walls give the scheme a contemporary feel, with large windows overlooking the street. Some residents have described it as the 'Costa del Bow' due to its similarity to Mediterranean housing with white rendered walls.

Design and construction

Donnybrook Quarter has been designed on a compact site next to two busy roads in a dense urban area. The plan of the site has been designed to maximise light and ensure that residents have a high degree of privacy. The scheme has well-designed terraces, front doors, bow windows and balconies overhanging the street. The design of Donnybrook Quarter was seen as a celebration of the public social life of the city.

Every aspect of the design is configured to promote buzzing, thriving public space made with a hard edge of buildings. Streets overlooked by balconies, bay windows and roof terraces. Streets where people might enjoy to sit out, kids to play, people going to and from their homes or just passing through.[97]

The development has a number of design precedents, from courtyard housing in Casablance by the Morrocan architect Jean-Francois Zevaco to courtyard housing in Evora by Alvaro Siza. Peter Barber describes the design as 'picturesque meets functionalism'.

↖ The single access road with a small public space at the rear.

↑ The design has allowed for retail units at the ground floor with apartments above.

← Ground-floor plan of Donnybrook Quarter.

Roads, parking and pedestrianisation

The central street is a quiet driveway of 7.5 metres width and bordered on each side by two-storey and three-storey buildings, giving the scheme a distinctive character. The central street is cycle, pedestrian and vehicle friendly but cars cannot park on the site. Instead, they have to park in the surrounding roads.

↑   Donnybrook maximises the site overlooking a busy junction.

→   The scheme has well-designed terraces, front doors, bow windows and balconies overhanging the street. The design of Donnybrook Quarter was seen as a celebration of the public social life of the city.

Environment and community

Trees have been planted to line the new central street and the construction of the walls exceeds insulation standards. The acrylic render system for the walls has enhanced environmental performance. There are a number of shops, which have been designed for local convenience and to give life to the street. Donnybrook has a mixed tenure with 21 per cent affordable housing and 5 per cent retail. The scheme provides residential accommodation for approximately 130 people in 40 units. There are apartments with one, two and three bedrooms, duplex apartments with two bedrooms, and a number of houses. There are three live/work units on Old Ford Road, each with two apartments.

Donnybrook Quarter, London

General

Site area 0.4 hectares	**Density** 400 habitable rooms per hectare
Total number of inhabitants/dwellings 130 people in 40 dwellings	**Housing mix by tenure** 21% affordable housing, 74% private housing
Average number of people per dwelling 2	**Percentage of commercial use** 5% (119m² workspace)

Character

	Objectives	Strengths	Weaknesses	Evaluation	Design quality standard
1.	Does the scheme feel like a place with a distinctive character?	Good distinctive character with a mix of heights and typology.	It is a shame it is such a small scheme and will be interesting to see how its character will be replicated on a bigger site.	A small scheme with well-designed spaces and street around existing roads give a distinctive character.	Good
2.	Do buildings exhibit architectural quality?	Good architectural design with good features, such as overhanging balconies and windows.	Colour has been well considered but it is a shame not to see more colour.	It will be interesting to see how this model will be replicated on bigger housing projects.	Very good
3.	Are streets defined by a coherent and well-structured layout?	One central street with dwellings on both sides.	—	This corner site has two existing streets to the external face of the site and an internal road which is well planned.	Good
4.	Do buildings and layout make it easy to find your way around?	The central street makes way finding straightforward.	—	It is a small site so way finding is not difficult.	Good
5.	Does the scheme exploit existing buildings, landscape or topography?	Good use of existing site with higher taller housing situated next to existing housing.	—	The massing of dwelling heights has been well-designed around existing buildings.	Good

Roads, parking and pedestrianization

6.	Does the building layout take priority over the roads and car parking, so that highways do not dominate?	—	—	The one central street does dominate the scheme but has been designed in such a way as to give the scheme character.	Good
7.	Are the streets pedestrian, cycle and vehicle friendly?	No cars can park on the central street but it is vehicle, pedestrian and cycle friendly.	—	The public street is pedestrian, cycle and vehicle friendly, but cars cannot park on the site.	Good
8.	Is car parking well-integrated so it supports the street scene?	—	No car parking on the site.	No parking on the site.	Good
9.	Does the scheme integrate with existing roads, paths and surrounding development?	The scheme is well-designed around existing streets and buildings.	—	Central street integrates well with existing roads.	Good
10.	Are public spaces and pedestrian routes overlooked and do they feel safe?	The public street feels safe.	—	The street is overlooked by the dwellings providing eyes to the street.	Good

Design and construction

	Objectives	Strengths	Weaknesses	Evaluation	Design quality standard
11.	Is the design specific to the scheme?	The scheme design is specific to the scheme and well-designed around existing streets and buildings.	—	Specific to the scheme but the design model could be built anywhere and later versions are being constructed presently in Tanner Street in the Thames Gateway.	Very good
12.	Is public space well-designed and does it have suitable management arrangements in place?	Well-planned central street with a statute at the far end.	The original plan shows public benches in the courtyard, which have not been constructed.	The scheme is part lease hold, part social rented, part freehold. The social part is housing association managed.	Very good
13.	Do buildings or spaces outperform statutory minima, such as building regulations?	The build-up of the walls and roofs exceeds insulation standards.	—	Careful thought has been given to save heat loss through the walls and roof.	Good
14.	Has the scheme made use of advances in construction or technology that enhance its performance, quality and attractiveness?	The acrylic render system for the walls enhances the performance due to the low maintenance.	The external white walls are looking as though they need a fresh coat.	The acrylic render system for the walls enhances the performance due to the low maintenance.	Average
15.	Do internal spaces and a layout allow for adaption, conversion or extension?	The internal spaces can be adapted for conversion.	—	The internal spaces can be adapted for conversion.	Average

Environment and community

	Objectives	Strengths	Weaknesses	Evaluation	Design quality standard
16.	Does the development have easy access to public transport?	Good bus links.	—	Good bus links, close to Victora park.	Good
17.	Does the development have any features that reduce its environmental impact?	Has good insulation and exceeds insulation standards.	There could be more features that reduce the environmental impact.	Careful thought has been given to save heat loss through the walls and roof.	Good
18.	Is there a tenure mix that reflects the needs of the local community?	Good tenure mix, well designed and caters for private and social housing.	There could be more social housing.	Good mix of accommodation with 21% affordable housing and 5% retail.	Good
19.	Is there a mix of accommodation that reflects the needs and aspirations of the local community?	A good mix of accommodation.	—	Good mix of accommodation with 21% affordable housing and 5% retail.	Good
20.	Does the development provide community facilities, such as a school, park play areas, shops, pubs or cafes?	A number of retail shops have been well designed and constructed at street level.	No new community facilities due to its small size.	The small site makes it difficult to provide such facilities but has a number of retail units that gives life to the street.	Good

chapter three

Learning from the Netherlands

Context

While we continue to treat architecture as a marginalised 'add-on', quantity will always prevail over quality, mammon over imagination. To construct cities around the belief that urban design and the public realm can be considered once land deals, planning policy and economic viability have been settled, is to submit our cities to a form of vandalism from which few will recover.[1]

Chapters 1 and 2 have attempted to ascertain the background to the question at the start of this book – why new housing in the United Kingdom is held to be so uninspiring. The case studies illustrate that there are many good-quality new housing projects in both the UK and the Netherlands that are attractive, robust, sustainable and ultimately habitable for generations to come. The social, cultural and political circumstances surrounding design quality in these two countries, however, are complex. This makes it difficult to compare the background and built examples of new housing. It is possible, however, to evaluate a number of common aspects.

This chapter will assess these common aspects on the basis of the findings of chapters 1 and 2, and make recommendations for design quality in new housing. The findings have been broken down into four areas of design quality under the following headings:

1. Methods of implementing design quality.
2. Design quality through spatial, social and cultural diversity.
3. Design quality through architectural and sustainable design.
4. Design quality through urban design.

Methods of implementing design quality

The prevailing observation in chapters 1 and 2 of this book is that good design quality results from a strong urban planning programme that has been well defined at the early stage of a housing development. Design quality has also been the result of a working relationship between the design team, planning department, quality team, developers, housing agencies and local authorities.

Furthermore, good design quality is the result of learning lessons from mistakes and successes of previously constructed housing projects. Examples of this can be observed in new housing schemes in the Netherlands, for example where the design and construction of each district of the Eastern Harbour District was completed in phased stages to allow problems to be defined and resolved for the development of the next phase. During the Java District project, lessons have been learnt from the previous district of KNSM Island, and lessons were provided for the later district of Borneo-Sporenburg. The success of the design of Vathorst can be attributed to the lessons learnt from the neighbouring districts of Kattenbroek and Nieweland that were built from 1990 to 1996 and 1995 to 2001 respectively.

Another successful method of implementing good design quality is the Dutch policy of individual commissioning. This enables individuals to develop more control over the quality of their own house and endows housing developments with architecturally lively, playful and colourful neighbourhoods.

In Vathorst, quality was achieved by a coherent design quality strategy framework, which was established at the outset of the design. Quality was also driven by a 'quality team', which was put together to cover four separate categories:

1. Maintenance of public space.
2. Specialist city design.
3. Architectural design.
4. Sustainability.[2]

This quality team, made up of architects, planners, built environment professionals and academics, was appointed on the basis of experience and knowledge. The quality team met once a month with a coordinating supervisor and with the city planner of Amersfoort. The quality team assessed if and to what extent the four quality categories were being implemented, and established a framework of design quality, which defined a number

↓   A detail of the façade of the Lighthouse.

↘   Careful detailing and contemporary design at the Abode,
Newhall, Harlow.

of targets and methods under which the best quality could be enforced. The partnership contractual model that was established was a split 50/50 stake in the design and construction between the municipality of Amersfoort and five development companies. This meant the risk was jointly shared and quality was evaluated by both principal roles. The group also monitored the city planner of Amersfoort, to assess whether he was consistent in his work and his quality targets were being met.

Shareholders of the five development companies had a part to play in the quality of the development. Design quality was discussed in yearly meetings between the shareholders, the development company and the quality team. The public were also invited to attend these yearly meetings and were invited to give opinions on the proposed development. The bilateral relationship between the city of Amersfoort and the quality team meant that the quality team had a more refined role than in other towns in the Netherlands. This further resulted in the quality team having more power to ensure that design quality was enforced.

It can also be observed that in the development of Ijburg an independent supervisory quality team and a quality plan were

established at the outset of the project. This team was headed by an experienced former Dutch government architect, Kees Rijnboutt, who coordinated the work of different architects and design professionals with a supervising team consisting of the architects Felix Claus, Frits Palmboom, Michael van Gassel, Jaap van den Bout, the urban planner Ton Schaap, the landscape architect Micheal van Gessel and the chairman of the aesthetic control commission Aart Oxenaar. Each architect and designer was appointed to a housing scheme and placed under the supervision of a block principal named a 'coach', who supervised the design and construction process of a specified housing block. The coach had to report at regular meetings to demonstrate that the design was within the quality target of the urban masterplan. All the designs were further analysed by a government amenities inspectorate and an independent expert design panel. Thus, quality in the design was rationalised through a series of checking processes. The architecture critic Hans Ibelings believes that the design of Ijburg typifies Dutch consensus as no single party has overall power and all parties including architects, contractors and developers have had to work together as one team. Ibelings maintains this has resulted in a system of 'checks and balances' and has guaranteed architectural and urban quality.[3]

A quality team was also appointed for the design of the Eastern Harbour District. This team was coordinated by a supervising architect in collaboration with a municipal urban planner, a member of the Urban Aesthetics Committee and a member of the Heritage Committee. The quality team prepared a *visual quality plan* document as a design tool to ensure that the quality of the submitted drawings was in accordance with urban planning targets. This visual quality plan was produced for the design of Java Island by Soeter Soeters and covered housing design, urban design and the management of public space. Architectural guidelines were also defined and a design quality strategy was developed for the public space with regards to the furnishing and ambience, paving material, types of trees, greenery, street furniture and lighting. The supervisor was able to guide all the architects in such a way that they could strengthen the original conceptual ideas of the designs and that good design ideas were not rejected. He did this by regular meetings and close collaboration with the architects and quality team. A visual quality plan was also prepared in a similar way for the other districts on the Eastern Harbour District.

In the case studies of new housing developments in the United Kingdom, the good implementation of design quality can also be attributed to a strong planning programme with a dedicated design team, planning department and local authority, which all have evaluated and monitored quality throughout the design and construction of the new housing scheme. The successful design of Accordia was a direct result of a combination of an imaginative city council with the planning department and

↙   An innovative approach to a private courtyard on Ijburg.

→   A design study of new housing in Ijburg by Palmboom and Van den Bout Architects.

remarkably simple: a strong planning department which forces a property developer into hiring a good master planner and a few talented practices.'[5]

The success of quality at Donnybrook Quarter, it can be observed, can be attributed to a combination of the commitment and vision of a creative housing association (Circle 33), of Hackney Council Planning Department and of the architect, Peter Barber Architects. The strength of the design is due to the rigour and commitment of those who initiated and joined the competition, which attracted many international entries.[6] Successful design quality in the Staiths can be attributed to a forward-thinking Gateshead Council with a creative planning department and designer. It is also largely as a result of the foresight and risk of the housebuilder, George Wimpey, to employ a designer who was inexperienced in housing to demonstrate that it is possible to construct a model of quality new housing. From the success of the case studies in the United Kingdom it becomes evident that commitment and hard work guarantees good results.

The case studies in this book all demonstrate that design codes, if utilised successfully, can help deliver better design quality with higher standards. The use of design codes for the Greenwich Millennium Village, the Eastern Harbour District and Vathorst shows that design codes can help implement a consistency and increase certainty in decision-making and the design strategy across the entire masterplan, whilst ensuring that individual housing projects are well designed.

Design coding should define urban infrastructure, public spaces, parking and street design. However, a balance has to be struck between the harmony achieved by design codes and the room needed for good design. The design code should not stifle good design but instead encourage and further the quality of a housing development.

Design codes nevertheless are still rarely used in new housing developments. Research carried out by Matthew Carmona demonstrates that codes are still used infrequently on the majority of new housing developments, with 73 per cent of respondents of a survey on the use of design coding in new housing stating they had not used design codes.[7] Those who used the codes were largely local authorities who stated that there is a need for the codes as a solution to dealing with challenges of particular sites, such as large brownfield sites, sites in sensitive locations and sites that have rough and unlevelled ground.

a good design team. Ellis Woodman, writing in *Building Design*, stated that Accordia was the first British version of 'exemplary housing projects that have been built on the edge of Dutch cities over the past decade'.[4] Alain de Botton, writing in the letters page of *Building Design*, pinpointed the success of Accordia as the result of a few key factors; 'The ingredients for success are

de erven (5)

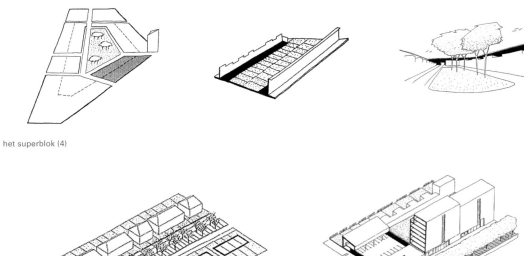
het superblok (4)

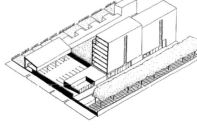

de modaalstraat

de parkrand

A winning formula?

In a letter to the *Architects' Journal*,[8] Julie Greer, manager of the design and conservation team of the London Borough of Southwark, provides a four-point formula for the successful implementation of design quality in the UK:

1. A good client who is committed to achieving high quality standards.
2. A well-resourced architectural team that can work with the local authority.
3. A good design officer and forward-thinking planning committee, willing to take risks.
4. On completion, a good management structure with local ownership.[9]

In summary, the quality of new housing projects is the result of a balance of a good design team, the intervention of the local authority, a committed planning committee and client. This balance, however, is largely determined by different parties having a shared understanding of design quality. It is vital that the appointed team for a new housing development sign up to a defined understanding of the meaning of design quality for each project. This framework for implementing design quality will be different for every housing development depending on the surrounding circumstances of the size, contract and type of housing. Quality teams need first to establish what design quality for their housing development means, second to create a framework of quality targets and third to adhere to those targets.

As has been discussed in chapter 2, according to the architect Richard Rogers the answer to further new housing in the United Kingdom is through the appointment of architects and design professionals to positions of power. Ian Abley, however, is against this concept as he states it will only benefit those architects themselves and not the quality of housing. It can be observed in this book, however, that the successful design and delivery of good quality housing is rather through a balance of appointing key architects, landscape architects, urban planners, designers and other built environment professionals within quality teams. These teams can ensure much more effectively that new housing has developed the appropriate level of design quality factors and that quality is established throughout the implementation and design process.

Size of typical floor areas in the Netherlands and the United Kingdom case studies compared with Parker Morris standards

	Lowest	Highest
Parker Morris standards		
Apartment	44.6m² (2 persons)	86.4m² (6 persons)
House	74.3m² (4 person, 2-storey centre terraced house)	97.5m² (6 person, 3-storey house)
Case study houses in the Netherlands		
Vathorst	100m²	500m²
Ypenburg apartments	110m²	110m²
Ypenburg houses	140m²	180m²
United Kingdom		
GMV apartments	52m²	90m²
Staiths	46.9 m² (apartments)	130m² (houses)
Accordia apartments	45m²	145m²
Accordia houses	90m²	350m²
£60,000 house (2 bedrooms)	76.5m²	76.5m²

Design quality through spatial, social and cultural diversity

Context

The Fifth National Policy Document on Spatial Planning places high importance on spatial diversity, cultural diversity and social equality. The CABE Housing Audit and Building for Life Standard touch briefly on these interconnected aspects of spatial, social and cultural diversity, but it is Dutch government policy that has defined these factors as vital to the success of design quality. The case studies in this book show that in some, but not in all, cases this diversity is implemented in practice.

Space standards

Internal space size in new housing is a significant factor in achieving good design quality. New housing is still being built to low space standards. Minimum space standards in the United Kingdom have been set as part of publicly funded housing programmes. Apart from the mandatory enforcement of Parker Morris Standards that were abolished in 1981, space standards have never been established as general requirements through the planning system or Building Regulations.

Many local authorities and planning departments in the United Kingdom still do not regard space standards as important in the design of new housing. This is highlighted in the Greater London Authority 2006 publication *Housing Space Standards*, which maintains that before 2004 space standards had never been applied via the planning system as the British government specifically discouraged their use.[10] Even, today, the report states that Kensington and Chelsea is the only London Borough that includes specific minimum standards for sizes of rooms.[11] As a result, the Greater London Authority report sets out a number of baseline standards of minimum internal dwelling areas in which the authority encourages London boroughs to modify their planning application forms to seek standards in five key areas: (1) design occupancy of dwellings (number of bed spaces); (2) aggregate floor area of cooking/eating/living areas of each dwelling; (3) individual bedroom floor areas of each dwelling; (4) floor area of built-in storage cupboards; (5) net internal dwelling floor area.[12]

The case studies in the United Kingdom have lower space standards than in the Netherlands. The table above illustrates that the size of new apartments and houses of the majority of case studies in this book, exceed Parker Morris standards, the most commonly cited benchmark for space standards. Furthermore,

in line with research by the RIBA, the Dutch housing developments have larger floor areas than their British equivalents.

It is revealing that the British government have awarded the Greenwich Millennium Village housing a Building for Life 'Gold' standard for design quality, yet it possesses the smallest typical unit areas out of all of the case studies and is relatively small in scale compared with new housing developments in the Netherlands.

The quality of new housing is dependent on the typical size of dwellings. A balance needs to be struck between implementing controls such as the proposal of baseline standards of minimum internal dwelling areas, density and the requirements and needs of functionality and value.

Density

Density is an essential factor for the design of new housing. Dutch and British government planning policies both promote increases in the density of new housing developments in existing urban areas, in particular where there is good transport infrastructure.

The case studies in this book all promote a variety of densities, ensuring social cohesion and visual diversity. The design of the Eastern Harbour District hosts a mixture of densities with larger apartment blocks planned around smaller low-rise terraced dwellings, achieving an average of 100 dwellings per hectare across the site. Ijburg also has a mixture of densities, with larger housing blocks and smaller individual housing. Vathorst, Leidsche Rijn and Ypenburg all have similar densities around 40 dwellings per hectare. However, in some neighbourhoods density varies in the same neighbourhood, such as in De Laak in Vathorst. In Leidsche Rijn, the masterplan was divided into two different densities – a northern strip with high densities and a southern field for low densities. Accordia and the Staiths have a mid range of densities with 65 and 58 dwellings per hectare respectively, comparable with the densities of many Dutch housing projects. The Greenwich Millennium Village has a high density at 220 dwellings per hectare.

Increasing the density of housing does not necessarily lead to better design quality. The Calcutt Review argues that if density is increased, the design must be accompanied by enhanced standards of space, amenity and management services that are enforceable through the planning system.[13] Once those standards are agreed at a national and local level, they should form part of the planning brief for the site. Density should not just be interpreted as an invitation to achieving a maximum price for a site. The Greater London Authority in the 2006 publication

Housing Space Standards contends that although notions of increased density can lead to good design it has also lead developers to interpret increased density as a reduction in dwelling size.[14] As a result, developers are constructing many small one- and two-bedroom flats. This is under a process of change, however, as English Partnerships are introducing minimum standards for flats.

As one of the consequences of the search to maximise floor sizes, storage space has been reduced. Karn and Sheridan state that storage space has been the main casualty in new housing developments.[15] This is due to the pressure to maximise dwelling sizes on as small a building footprint as possible. The Greater London Authority's *Housing Space Standards* states that there is an emerging trend for smaller size dwellings even though house buyers have expressed a preference for larger, more flexible space.[16] Both the Dutch and British case studies demonstrate

a trend toward a lack of adequate storage space. In the Staiths housing development, the residents complained of a lack of storage,[17] as was also the case in the Eastern Harbour District.[18]

The needs and aspirations of the community

The CABE Housing Audit and the Dutch government's Fifth National Spatial Policy both highlight the importance of providing housing that reflects the needs and aspirations of the community. In the design of the Dutch case studies the needs of the community have been well considered and actively supported.

At Vathorst, the master planners and quality team sought to create a balance of contemporary housing and what they defined as 'classical' housing, which is housing in a traditional style. After conducting surveys of the type of housing that potential residents wanted to live in, it was established that new housing occupiers prefer to live in a house with traditional or 'classical' style rather than a contemporary house. The development team at Vathorst, however, decided against building an entire housing development in the traditional style of housing. Instead, a balance was sought between a mixture of contemporary housing and more traditional style. Although it was known that the 'classical' style houses were in higher demand and would sell for higher prices, the quality team and the architects wanted to create contemporary and innovative housing. The 5,000 terraced contemporary houses of the De Laak area of Vathorst by West 8 Architects were designed and built with the knowledge that they would be less profitable than 'classical' detached equivalents. The risk, however, was accepted in the drive for a district of high quality designed houses. The consumer's wishes were known and yet the city of Amersfoort pushed for higher principles of design quality.

The difference in Vathorst from most new housing developments in the United Kingdom is that the housing consumer was not given a prescribed housing type that it was assumed the residents would like or buy. Instead a balance was struck between the wishes of the consumer and the long-term quality of the development.

In the design for the Staiths, the housebuilder sought to involve the community in the design process. Community representatives attended regular design team meetings on topics such as waste disposal and public transport. One outcome of these meetings was the introduction of landscaped and concealed communal bin stores. For the majority of people interviewed at the Staiths the housing was as good as or better than they had expected once they lived there. Residents' reasons for buying at the Staiths were primarily the design at 49 per cent, followed by location at 34 per cent, which residents chose over affordability at 25 per cent and value for money at 21 per cent. Design was the most highly rated reasons for choosing the house as residents liked the contemporary, spacious open plan with big windows and good details. Resident satisfaction was reported to be 'high' at 38 per cent, 'reasonably high' at 43 per cent and 'low' at 2 per cent. Residents disliked the lack of storage within the houses, small bedrooms, no garages, small bathrooms, poor workmanship such as leaking roofs, squeaky floors, brickwork and thin ceilings. Some residents criticised the lack of local infrastructure, such as good schools and few facilities.[19]

In Vathorst, three schools were constructed in a group, at the same time as the first houses and completed before most residents had moved in. The community buildings and infrastructure were planned early so that the first residents did not lack any facilities. The shopping centre was considered secondary in priority and was started on site in 2007, five years after the first houses were constructed. In Ijburg and Ypenburg, an economic and social centre was constructed with a main station, shopping facilities and a large pedestrian square.

In its evaluation of the Netherlands, the Calcutt Review states that the good quality of housing in the Netherlands results in stronger communities compared to those in the UK.[20] This is supported by evidence from a survey that was held among the current population of Vathorst. In the Netherlands it is common practice for local councils to publish satisfaction ratings for housing residents. In Vathorst, a yearly report of housing statistics is published by the City Council of Amersfoort, containing a survey of every new housing development in the surrounding municipality.[21] The survey, which questioned the population of Vathorst on behalf of the development agency OBV, was sent to all 3,000 homes requesting them to take part in the questionnaire. Seventy-eight per cent of the residents who responded were very satisfied with the housing development and satisfied with the provision of primary schools in the area. Social cohesion in the neighbourhood is high at a 62 per cent rating out of 100 percent.[22] Eighty-four per cent of residents were satisfied with their house in Vathorst.[23] Fifty-two per cent of residents were satisfied about play areas for children. Residents were very satisfied with their neighbourhood overall at 75 per cent. Residents also praised the quality of the environment and gave an overall satisfaction rating of 72 per cent.[24] A number of the respondents took part in a larger group discussion at the neighbourhoods of De Velden and De Laak. The United Kingdom could learn from measuring satisfaction ratings of residents such as in the Netherlands rather than using a defined list of factors.

The Calcutt Review suggests that design quality in the United Kingdom should be measured by customer satisfaction and not by a subjective set of criteria.[25] It recommends that a new assessment should be developed with the Building for Life standard as a starting point but be extended to be viable for both larger housing developments and for individual building. This proposal takes into account the requirements of the residents rather than the requirements of a judging panel. Every new housing development in the Netherlands conducts a survey to establish whether the residents are satisfied with their new environment.

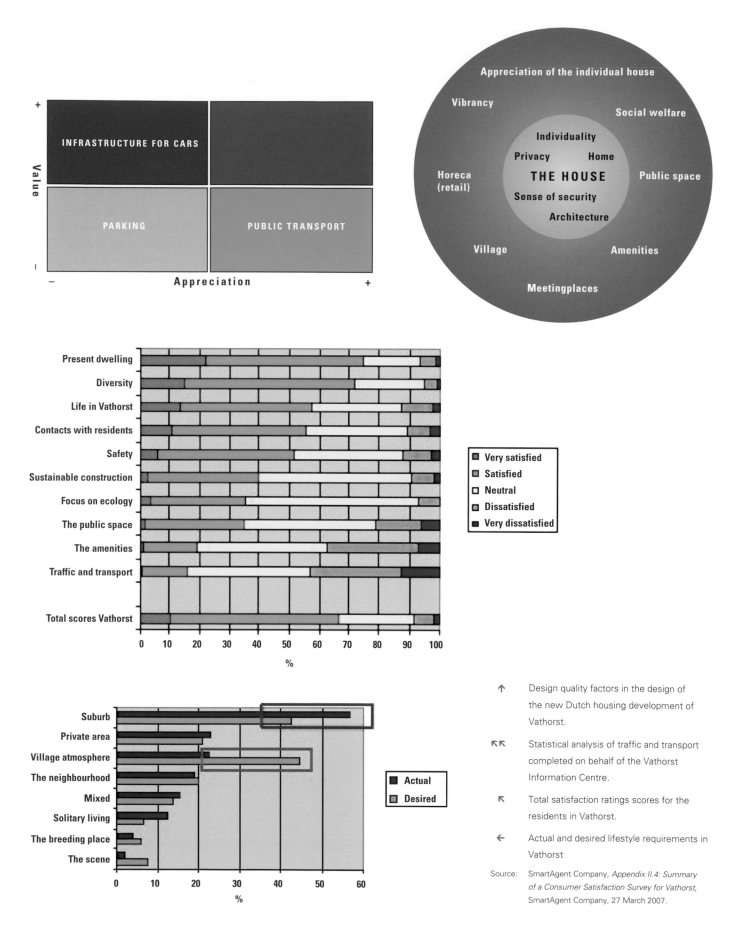

↑ Design quality factors in the design of the new Dutch housing development of Vathorst.

↖↖ Statistical analysis of traffic and transport completed on behalf of the Vathorst Information Centre.

↖ Total satisfaction ratings scores for the residents in Vathorst.

← Actual and desired lifestyle requirements in Vathorst

Source: SmartAgent Company, *Appendix II.4: Summary of a Consumer Satisfaction Survey for Vathorst*, SmartAgent Company, 27 March 2007.

Design quality through architectural and sustainable design

Context

Architectural design in the Netherlands has been promoted through the Dutch government's architecture and national spatial policies. Dutch architecture policy has implemented a number of architecture centres, prizes and awards that raise an awareness of good housing in the Netherlands. The British government has not drafted a national architecture policy to date. However, in October 2001 the Scottish Executive published *A Policy on Architecture* for Scotland, which has been widely regarded.[26] This publication has not been developed further for the rest of the United Kingdom. Innovative local authorities have introduced policies to raise quality and to integrate housing in their existing context. The Essex Design Guide was the best-known attempt of this. This is used as a model for the implementation of design quality in many local authorities in England and Wales.

CABE has been given increased funding to provide greater support in delivering high quality housing. CABE claims that through public campaigns and support to professionals it can encourage better design quality. CABE as a body does raise awareness and has set design quality targets and highlighted poor quality housing. However, one can question the effectiveness in relation to the improvement of the standard of housing in the United Kingdom. An example of this is the £60,000 house.

The concept of the £60,000 house demonstrates that the British government has recognised that design quality is important and can be improved. In the design brief for the competition, the Department of Trade and Industry compares the design of the £60,000 house to the ambitions of the Garden City towns of the 1920s. It is difficult, however, to compare the balanced quality of the Garden Cities with the construction of the £60,000 house and its associated housing scheme. Furthermore, each dwelling has minimum dimensions at an average of 76.5 square metres and the development lacks the associated community facilities, shops and landscaping. The 2005 publication *The Role and Effectiveness of CABE* by the House of Commons stated the £60,000 price should not be at the cost of creating poorly designed homes that will not last; also, CABE should be given a clear role in vetting the schemes.[27] The cost is an important part of the design of the £60,000 house, however, what has been lost is the quality of the housing development as a whole. The scheme demonstrates that the British government needs to concentrate, instead, on delivering and monitoring the implementation of design quality within new housing development projects by ensuring that the government and CABE can work together to raise the average quality of the many new housing projects that will be constructed in the United Kingdom. This means establishing effective control mechanisms, which provide incentives and support, and enforce quality in the design process until and beyond construction.

Architectural design

The case studies in this book illustrate that many housing projects that have been constructed in the Netherlands are of very high quality, and typically high-density low-rise buildings, interspersed with larger density blocks. The design of the new districts is characterised by a variety of colourful forms and styles and can be described as a combination of a 'vernacular' and functionalist style. Many individual houses such as in Ijburg, Vathorst and the Eastern Harbour District are distinct from each other and differ in massing, internal spatial arrangements and treatment of façades.

All the case studies show successful design of private, semi-public and public spaces. Courtyards are quiet, car-free and designed for the pedestrian and children. A key feature of Borneo-Sporenburg is the reinterpretation of the traditional house. The design of the 'mews court' on Ijburg and Vathorst with a combined area for vehicles and pedestrian access is successful in that it creates a quiet zone behind the street.

The success of the architectural design in Borneo-Sporenburg derives from its initial conceptual design of high density, low rise. This was not the lowest tendered bid but the design was held to be the most unique and offered for the existing site the most interesting and best design. In the Eastern Harbour District and Ijburg most dwellings have been well designed with a view of the surrounding basin and sea. At Vathorst, Leidsche Rijn and Ypenburg many views have been designed so they overlook lakes, dykes and fields. Important contextual features in the distance act as views, vistas and landmarks like a Japanese garden or the garden cities, which have been designed around an axis with landmarks, which further enhances diversity.

A feature of the design of the internal spaces in the case studies has been the provision of high ceiling heights. This provides more of a feeling of space within the dwelling and allows light to penetrate deep into the internal spaces. The design of the Eastern Harbour District and Ijburg included ground floor ceiling heights designed at 3.5 metres high. In Accordia ceiling heights were designed at 3 metres high. The actual width of dwellings in the case studies is relatively narrow. In Accordia the plots are 5.2 metres wide, and 5.4 metres in the Eastern Harbour District. One method of implementing good design quality in the UK is the enforcement of a standard for ceiling heights and plot widths through a design code or within an urban plan.

All the housing schemes in the case studies within this book have been designed with a diverse urban identity. The diversity of each housing project has enhanced the environment and has attracted residents and businesses to buy or rent properties. The diverse range of dwelling sizes promotes a mix of social groups and avoids social segregation. All the case studies have managed to provide well-designed public and semi-public spaces. The implementation of design codes and a more effective use of a masterplan are vital to the delivery of a diverse housing development. They provide consistency and coherence while allowing flexibility for individual housing designs to provide a pattern of varied colour, forms and styles.

It becomes apparent from the case studies in the Netherlands that it is the constraints and restrictions that develop and enhance the design. In the Eastern Harbour District it was the rigidly applied plot sizes, and the requirement for the amount of void within the houses and design code, that enhanced the diversity of the proposals and the creativity of the architects and designers. In Ijburg, a strictly applied urban plan and quality

framework established a clear strategy towards individual housing blocks. In this respect, design intent should be able to follow the rigour of the urban plan.

Thus, it is clear that massing, block dimensions, proportions, plot sizes, and height are all important factors in the design of new housing schemes. Good design adds value to homes and creates an environment people will want to live in. This can be demonstrated at the Staiths, as Phase 1 of the development reportedly sold out within four hours of going on sale in January 2003. For the second release of homes, buyers queued overnight to ensure they would be able to buy the home of their choice. New dwellings on Borneo-Sporenburg also reportedly sold out within hours of going on sale. In Greenwich Millennium Village, over 80 per cent of residents have reported that they were influenced to buy their property because of its sustainable design features.[28]

Sustainable design

Sustainable design is vital to the design quality of new housing developments. There have been, however, differing approaches towards sustainable design in the case studies included in this book. Some of the housing developments have implemented very few sustainable features, other housing projects have developed innovative approaches to sustainable design with new underground separated refuse disposal systems, combined heat, power and wind turbines, systems of construction waste and increased biodiversity.

Learning from sustainable features implemented in Vathorst, it can be observed that sustainable design should be implemented at a macro and micro scale. On the macro scale sustainable design has been considered in a design code and within the master plan. It has been considered separately for each neighbourhood and for each house. On the micro scale, small details have been considered such as ensuring that swallow birds' nests in the eaves of the existing houses are retained, as well as retaining existing trees, hedges and road surfaces and specifying the right type of soil so that birds can graze.

It can be observed from the case studies that achieving good quality sustainable design comes from new housing developments setting their own standards towards sustainable design which aims to exceed building regulation standards. This has been achieved at both Vathorst and Accordia. The master plan and design code should set the standard of what the sustainable target should be and the design team should work towards this standard. This takes commitment and hard work to implement and monitor but is achievable. In Vathorst, the residents have been reported to highly appreciate the efforts that have been made to preserve the natural plant and animal life and the policies that have led to reduced energy use. The British government has set the objective that by 2016 all new homes will be built to zero-carbon standards. In the Netherlands, however, new homes will be built to zero-carbon standards by 2020, four years later. Time will tell if the British government has been overly optimistic in its implementation of zero-carbon standards in new housing. Producing zero-carbon homes is estimated to cost up to 10 per cent more than typical homes. It can be observed from the Greenwich Millennium Village that sustainable housing costs more to build than typical housing. However, the case studies of new housing in the Netherlands demonstrate that the cost of sustainable design can be shared by the residents, development companies and shareholders. In Vathorst the majority of the inhabitants have been reported to be prepared to pay more money for sustainable construction methods[29].

Design quality through urban design

Context

Urban design is a vital but often overlooked characteristic of design quality. This is a broad category, which encompasses infrastructure, public space design, parking, road design, cycle lanes, landscaping and pedestrianization. In the Dutch case studies there has been a large programme of building railway lines and railway stations, such as in Ypenburg and Leidsche Rijn. These two developments were ideally placed next to major motorways and the A2 motorway at Leidsche Rijn was rerouted and designed with a sloping grass roof to reduce noise pollution and enable the town to be built adjacent to the motorway.

The successful delivery of infrastructure is important to the quality of new housing developments and will be critical to new housing projects in the Thames Gateway. Nicholas Falk, director of URBED, a cooperative specialising in urban design and regeneration, believes that the early investment of infrastructure in the Netherlands has contributed to the quality of new housing developments. He believes this is essential for new housing in the United Kingdom.

We simply will not be able to deliver what is expected in the Growth Areas without radical changes in the way we work together. The group thought that the people we met [in the Netherlands] had been more adventurous and learning from past mistakes. They seemed to be better at taking a team approach, and having a positive attitude and in maintaining spaces to higher standards...One of the main reasons for the Dutch success in building so many new homes has been their investment in infrastructure early on in ways that build confidence that plans will be implemented.[30]

The Dutch case studies demonstrate the importance of an early investment in infrastructure. The Dutch government provided four billion Euros for the Vinex housing programme of which 70–80 per cent was for infrastructure.[31] Most of the infrastructure was planned to be provided by the time a third of the housing was built. The Calcutt Review highlights that the funding of infrastructure in the Netherlands has been achieved by a combination of government investment and by pooling land, making a charge on developers when homes were completed. In some new housing districts the municipality charged developers on average 20 per cent of the sales value, going up to 28 per cent on more expensive homes.[32]

As Nicholas Falk rightly points out, the United Kingdom can learn lessons that infrastructure and community facilities need to be constructed at the same time as a housing project is built, or before it is completed.

Parking

Parking is a significant factor influencing the quality of new housing. The CABE Housing Audit stated that one of the most problematic features of poor design quality is parking and that poor

parking design is the key contributor to the majority of the schemes being assessed as poor. This is further evidenced in the case studies such as in Vathorst, where it was reported that a dominating concern of residents was the inadequacy of parking.[33]

In the document *Paving the Way* CABE highlights four main issues that affect parking for new housing developments:

1. Existing statute law, regulations and design guidance are out of tune with priority to streetscape.
2. Local highway authorities rely on standard practice.
3. The relative status of many statutes and documents of urban design is confused.
4. The powers given to local authorities in their role as highways authorities are often at odds with aims of planning and urban design.[34]

The design of new housing developments, therefore, should carefully implement a diversity of parking provision, with underground car parking, private parking and on-street parking. On Ijburg, for example, there is a range of underground car parking, on-street parking and private garages within the house, not as a separate component. If the site has physical constraints and is relatively high density it is good practice to design hidden underground parking contained within multi-storey basements and garages within housing blocks. This enables courtyards to be car-free, quiet and for the pedestrian. There should be some provision for on-street parking; however, the layout should not dominate the housing scheme. It can be observed from the Staiths that the exclusion of individual garages next to dwellings removes visual clutter and instead creates a good buffer for the provision of landscaping, trees and children's play areas.

A balance needs to be struck, therefore, between the number of car parking spaces for each dwelling and the physical requirements of car parking provision. The design and allocation of parking spaces needs to be implemented early on in a masterplan or design code.

↑   An innovative approach to car parking in Ypenburg.

↗   An example of a Home Zone in Vathorst consisting of large
        pavements with a wide cycle lane and a single road for cars.

Roads, pedestrianisation and cycling

The provision for roads, pedestrianisation and cycling is not often considered important to the quality of new housing. The case studies, however, illustrate that these factors are a vital feature of the visual and functional spaces between dwellings.

The motorway was one of the central features in the early design and masterplan of Leidsche Rijn. The A2 motorway was covered for a distance of two kilometres, with a landscaped roof containing recreation facilities including tennis courts and football pitches, housing and park areas.

The case studies have all implemented a grading of road sizes and widths. Thus, the design of Accordia includes quiet roads, which lead to a main road. In the Staiths, streets have been graded gradually and as a result the entrance road is a wide, busy two-lane avenue with cars and pedestrians separated by defined roads and pavements. The graded roads then become narrower and pavements become wider. New housing developments should implement the concept of the Home Zone. If implemented correctly, this creates safer, quieter roads in the centre of housing developments.

Most of the case studies have implemented bicycle lanes and pedestrian footpaths. A distinction has been made between smaller and larger cycle paths, some combined with road traffic routes. At Leidsche Rijn cycle lanes form a network of parallel grids across the site at 500 metres apart with a distinction made with smaller and larger cycle paths. In Vathorst, cycle lanes are as wide as the road for traffic, which has been reduced to a single lane in quieter residential streets.

Incentives should be given to residents to encourage the use of the bicycle. In the Staiths, cycling was encouraged by providing communal cycle sheds in communal courtyards and all residents were given £50 contribution towards the purchase of a bicycle.

Recommendations for implementing design quality in new housing

Implementation of design quality

1. What steps have been made to implement design quality within the brief, contract and interdisciplinary team relationships?
2. How has design quality been implemented within the urban design and planning process?
3. What measures has the team established to clarify their design quality within their roles and responsibilities?

Spatial, social and cultural diversity

4. Do the space standards reflect the needs of the occupier?
5. Are streets defined by a coherent and well planned layout?
6. Does the scheme exploit existing buildings, landscape or topography?
7. Is there a variety in the type and tenure of housing that reflects the needs of the local community?
8. Is there a mix of accommodation and community facilities that reflects the needs and aspirations of the local community?

Architectural and sustainable design

9. Do buildings or spaces outperform statutory minima, such as building regulations?
10. What design features are in place to reduce the environmental impact?
11. What lessons can the proposed housing scheme learn from sustainable design of similar previous housing projects?
12. Do buildings exhibit architectural quality?
13. Has the scheme made use of advances in construction or technology that enhance its performance, quality and attractiveness?
14. Does the scheme feel like a place with a distinctive character?
15. Does the housing scheme have any historical and cultural precedents?

Urban design

16. Does the infrastructure reflect the needs of the development and the community?
17. Is public space well-designed and does it have suitable management arrangements in place?
18. What reasons are behind the planning and implementation of density and design codes and how does this affect the quality of the design?
19. Does the development have easy access to public transport?
20. Are public spaces and pedestrian routes overlooked, are they well lit and do they feel safe?
21. Does the building layout take priority over the roads and car parking, so that highways do not dominate?
22. What measures have been made to make the streets pedestrian, cycle and vehicle friendly?
23. Are car parking and roads well-integrated so they support the street scene and surrounding development?

Coherence

24. How are all of these factors linked together in the design of the housing scheme?
25. Does the scheme exhibit coherence throughout the implementation, planning and design process?

Conclusions

This book has attempted to evaluate the design quality of new housing in the Netherlands and the United Kingdom. It has not been written to highlight the problems that occur in the design of new housing developments but, instead, has sought to provide an understanding of the complexities of what has been described as the 'sustainababble' and 'communitwaddle'[1] in new housing. It is acknowledged that the procurement, design and construction of new housing are demanding. It is also recognised that shaping of good design quality is complex and commercial pressures weigh against the time-consuming investment of implementing quality.

Housebuilders in the United Kingdom are largely profit-driven, in an industry characterised by commercial uncertainties, and the pressures of the market are often intense. In these circumstances, design quality is often marginalised as an insignificant part of the design process. If any characteristics of design quality are established it is usually after the design has already taken shape.

By learning from new housing in the Netherlands it can be ascertained that a few simple implementation procedures can help deliver better quality homes. Design quality must be sought at an early stage, with a committed team who has the experience and imagination to drive it. There has to be a clear and direct system of decision-making, which adheres to a strong urban planning programme. A quality team should be established with an obligation to further the quality of a housing scheme through shared goals within a coherent design strategy. An obligatory quality framework that provides a 'system of checks and balances' should be established for each housing development and then implemented and monitored throughout the scheme. Experts and specialists should be appointed to evaluate the framework to ensure quality is being enforced. The housing development, when completed, should establish an effective management policy as defined within the quality framework.

One of the reasons why new housing is so complex can be related to the plethora of separate and distinct values that different parties involved in the delivery and design of new housing have placed on design quality. An example of this is that CABE and the Building for Life programme assess design quality with a different set of criteria than planning policy. Design quality of new housing schemes in the Netherlands are instead assessed through resident satisfaction surveys, which allows a more accurate picture to be determined of the quality of housing. As a result a single, uniform assessment of design quality should be established that incorporates the majority of the complex interconnected factors of the design of new housing into a simple and easy-to-understand list of factors based on the needs and aspirations of residents and the community.

It is possible to argue that the methods of implementing design quality in the United Kingdom are not performing adequately. It is reported that the Design Quality Indicator assesses only 10 per cent of social housing and only 20 per cent of all projects in excess of £1million.[2] Furthermore, CABE states that it carries out design review assessments on only around 350 schemes per year and the majority of these assessments are not new housing developments.[3] Compared to the hundreds of thousands of new houses that are planned to be constructed in the United Kingdom, this represents a very small fraction of an effective framework of quality control for new housing.

The internal size of dwellings is a significant factor for design quality. Only one London borough includes specific minimum standards for internal sizes of dwellings, and before 2004 space standards had not been applied via the planning system as the government specifically discouraged their use. Mandatory minimum baseline space standards should be established that use Parker Morris Standards as a guideline and include floor areas and storage areas.

The case studies also demonstrate the importance of urban design. New housing developments should offer a variety of well-designed urban solutions for neighbourhoods such as a separation between public, semi-public and private spaces and courtyards, Home Zones, road layout, public space design, children's play areas and public landscaping. Parking policy and design needs to be radically rethought and examples such as in new housing projects in the Netherlands and the United Kingdom can be used as a precedent of what can be achieved with a diverse parking environment.

Architects, built environment professionals, local authorities and planning departments can learn many lessons from new housing in the Netherlands. Ricky Burdett, the former adviser on

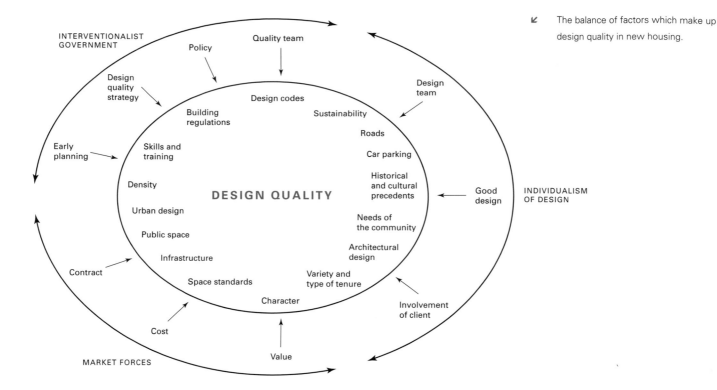

Within the diagram:

INTERVENTIONALIST GOVERNMENT

Policy — Quality team

Design quality strategy

Design codes

Building regulations — Sustainability

Design team

Early planning

Skills and training

Roads

Car parking

Density

DESIGN QUALITY

Historical and cultural precedents

Good design

INDIVIDUALISM OF DESIGN

Urban design

Needs of the community

Public space

Architectural design

Contract

Infrastructure

Space standards

Variety and type of tenure

Involvement of client

Cost

Character

MARKET FORCES

Value

architecture and urbanism to the Mayor of London, is correct in saying the design vision for the Thames Gateway in south-east England should be sought from the Netherlands. There is more government intervention both centrally and locally in the development of Dutch housing policy at an early stage of housing developments than in the United Kingdom.

The housing projects in this book predominantly demonstrate that good design quality is about achieving a balance. There is a fine line between state intervention and individualism of design. Market forces cannot be left alone to produce good quality housing. Individual design should flourish through a properly enforced and monitored urban planning framework. Architects and designers should be able to create innovative and expressive designs within established strict guidelines. Many new Dutch housing projects are of a better standard than in the United Kingdom due to more interventionist government guidelines, which control and monitor the design.

The Dutch have published a national architecture policy, which provides an effective framework of design quality objectives. The Scottish Executive has published an architecture policy for Scotland but currently there is no architecture policy for England and Wales. Examples of housing such as in Vathorst and at Accordia are evidence for the fact good housing schemes can be designed that residents are satisfied with, exceed building regulations, have clear sustainable objectives and are attractive. Vathorst is evidence that if shareholders, residents and developers have greater incentives to create better design quality they will be prepared to pay more for quality if it means higher standards of sustainable design, space standards and a more socially

cohesive community. This extra cost will be reimbursed, as the housing scheme is marketable, popular and long lasting.

Ultimately, design quality should be used as a key negotiating tool. If a housing scheme lacks the basic elements of design quality described in this book, it should not gain planning approval. Design quality is not achieved with a checklist of afterthoughts. It is not a series of standards. It is much more than this. It is matching the aspirations of those individuals, parties and stakeholders involved in the whole, continuing process of the planning, design, construction and management of a particular housing development. Durability, attractiveness and satisfaction of each individual house and the coherence of an entire scheme can only be achieved if they are established from early and clear methods.

By achieving a balance of design quality the average standard of the low- and high-rise doll's houses and Dan Dare steel and glass towers that will be built on the Thames Gateway, the new eco-towns and the three million new homes in the United Kingdom can be raised.

Good design quality in the many new housing projects in the future is, therefore, achievable. However, how it is implemented is essentially down to every one of us; we all have a say and a voice to shape the built environment that we live in. Design quality can help to achieve the needs and aspirations of the community and goals and ambitions of the designers, architects, planners and policy makers. As the housing developments in the Netherlands demonstrate, good design quality is there for the taking.

Notes

Introduction

1   Royal Institute of British Architects, *Better Homes and Neighbourhoods*, RIBA Policy Paper, London, 2007, p. 4.

2   Commission for Architecture and the Built Environment, *The Housing Audit, Assessing the Design Quality of New Homes*, London: CABE Publications, 2004.

3   Commission for Architecture and the Built Environment, *The Housing Audit for the North East, North West and Yorkshire and Humber in the UK*, London: CABE Publications, 2005.

4   VROM, *General Data*, 2007. Online. Available HTTP: <http://international.vrom.nl/pagina.html> (accessed 31 August 2007).

5   L. Clarke and C. Wall, *Skills and the Construction Process: A Comparative Study of the Vocational Training and Quality in Social Housebuilding*, Bristol: The Policy Press, 1996, p. 79.

6   M. Ball, *A Troubled Relationship*, Bristol: The Policy Press, 1998, p. 76.

7   W. Hemingway, 'One Staiths South Bank: A Dynamic New Concept in Housing', *Wimpey Homes Homelife*, 2006.

8   E. Heathcote, 'What's So Good About British Architecture', *Financial Times*, 1 September 2007.

9   R. Rogers and M. Fisher, *A New London*, London: Penguin, 1992, p. xxx

10 Urban Task Force, *Towards an Urban Renaissance: Final Report of the Urban Task Force*, London: Spon Press, 1999.

11 Ibid., p. 32.

12 R. Rogers, *Housing for a Compact City*, London: GLA Architecture and Urbanism Unit, 2000.

13 'Modern methods of construction' refers to a variety of innovative build approaches using products and techniques aimed at improving efficiency in construction. They include off-site manufacturing and improved management methods imported from the construction sector. This approach was used for the construction of the Greenwich Millennium Village and the Summit Townhouse.

14 R. Burdett, 'More Vision Needed for Thames Gateway', *Building Design*, 21 January 2005, p. 5.

15 W. Hemmingway, 'Time for the Ultimate Home Makeover', *Society Guardian*, 14 June, 2002.

16 Deputy Prime Minister's Construction Task Force, 1998, cited in D. Gann, *Flexibility and Choice in Housing*, Bristol: The Policy Press, 1999, p. 24.

17 M. Carmona, S. Carmona and N. Gallent, *Delivering New Homes: Processes, Planners and Providers*, London: Routledge, 2003, p. 121.

18 The Housing Corporation, *Design and Quality Strategy*, London: The Housing Corporation 2007.

19 Home Builders Federation, Crown Copyright, *Calcutt Review of Housebuilding Delivery: Submission by Home Builders Federation*, London: HBF, 2007.

20 M. Carmona, *Housing Design Quality, Through Policy, Guidance and Review*, London: Spon Press, 2001, pp. 141–142.

21 M. Carmona, *Delivering New Homes: Processes, Planners and Providers*, London: Routledge, 2003, p. 223.

22 Ministry of Housing, Spatial Planning and the Environment Communication Directorate, *Making Space, Sharing Space: Fifth National Policy Document on Spatial Planning 2000/2020*, The Hague, 2001, p. 5.

23 Llewelyn Davies, *Urban Design Compendium*, London: Llewelyn Davies, 2000; Commission for Architecture and the Built Environment, *Design Review: How CABE Evaluates Quality in Architecture and Urban Design*, London: CABE Publications, 2006; Commission for Architecture and the Built Environment, *Housing Audit: Assessing the Design Quality of New Homes*, London: CABE Publications, 2004; Department for Transport, Local Government and the Regions/CABE, *By Design: Better Places to Live: A Companion Guide to PPG3*, Tonbridge: Thomas Telford, 2001

24 Commission for Architecture and the Built Environment, *Design Review: How CABE Evaluates Quality in Architecture and Urban Design*, London: CABE Publications, 2006, p. 14.

25 Ibid.

26 Sunand Prasad, 'Measuring Quality and Value: Inclusive Maps', in S. Macmillan, *Designing Better Buildings, Quality and Value in the Built Environment*, London: Spon Press, 2003, p. 182.

One
Design quality in the Netherlands

1   VROM, *General Data*, 2007. Online. Available HTTP: <http://international.vrom.nl/pagina.html> (accessed 31 August 2007).

2   H. Baldock, 'Thinking Big', *Building Design*, 8 September 2000, p. 28.

3   A. Wortmann, 'Kattenbroek and Ypenburg', *Archis*, 3, 2003.

4   VROM, *Housing Production and Renovation*, 2007. Online. Available HTTP: <http://international.vrom.nl/pagina.html> (accessed 31 August 2007).

5   H. Ibelings, *The Artificial Landscape: Contemporary Architecture, Urbanism, and Landscape Architecture in the Netherlands*, Rotterdam: NAI Publishers, 2000, p. 195.

6   H. Vuijste and M. T. Hooker, *The Politically Correct Netherlands since the 1960s*, Westport, CT: Greenwood Press, 2000.

7   A. Betsky, *False Flat: Why Dutch Design is So Good*, London: Phaidon, 2004, p. 34.

8   P. Boelhouwer, 'The Disfunctionality of the Dutch Housing Market: Exploding House Prices Versus Falling Housing Production', paper presented at the ENHR conference, Cambridge, July 2004, p. 7.

9   H. Ibelings, *The Artificial Landscape: Contemporary Architecture, Urbanism, and Landscape Architecture in the Netherlands*, Rotterdam: NAI Publishers, 2000, p. 11.

10   B. Lootsma, *SuperDutch: New Architecture in the Netherlands*, London: Thames and Hudson, 2000.

11   H. Ibelings, *The Artificial Landscape: Contemporary Architecture, Urbanism, and Landscape Architecture in the Netherlands*, Rotterdam: NAI Publishers, 2000.

12   A. Zaero-Polo, 'A Scientific Autobiography', *Harvard Design Magazine*, fall 2004/winter 2005, p. 9.

13   VROM, *Housing, Spatial Planning and the Environment*, 2007. Online. Available HTTP: <http://www.sharedspaces.nl/pagina.html?id=7328> (accessed 31 August 2007).

14   VROM, 2007. Online. Available HTTP: <http://international.vrom.nl/pagina.html> (accessed 31 August 2007).

15   Ministry of Housing, Spatial Planning and the Environment Communication Directorate, *Making Spaces, Sharing Space*: *Fifth National Policy on Spatial Planning, 2000/2020l* The Hague, 2001, p. 9.

16   H. Van Dijk, 'Anarchical Housing Consumers', *Architecture in the Netherlands Yearbook 1998–1999*, Rotterdam: NAI Publishers, 1999, p. 14.

17   H. Van Dijk, 'Anarchical Housing Consumers', *Architecture in the Netherlands Yearbook 1998–1999*, Rotterdam: NAI Publishers, 1999.

18   Education, Culture and Science, Housing, Spatial Planning and the Environment, Transport, Public Works and Water Management, Agriculture, Nature Management and Fisheries, *Architectural Policy 2001–2004: The Architecture of Space: Shaping the Netherlands*, The Hague: Education, Culture and Science, Housing, Spatial Planning and the Environment, Transport, Public Works and Water Management, Agriculture, Nature Management and Fisheries, 2001.

19   Housing, Spatial Planning and the Environment, *Designing in the Netherlands*, The Hague: Housing, Spatial Planning and the Environment, Communication Directorate, 2000.

20   Ministry of Housing, Spatial Planning and the Environment Communication Directorate, *Making Spaces, Sharing Space*: *Fifth National Policy on Spatial Planning, 2000/2020l*, The Hague, 2001, p. 9.

21   Ibid., p. 5.

22   VROM, *Housing Production and Renovation*, 2007. Online. Available HTTP: <http://international.vrom.nl/pagina.html> (accessed 31 August 2007).

23   Netherlands Institute for Spatial Research, *Vinex: A Morphological Exploration*, Rotterdam/Den Haag: NAI Publishers, 2006. Online. Available HTTP: <http://www.rpb.nl/en-gb/> (accessed 13 December 2007).

24   An example of this was when the national newspaper the *NRC Handelsblad* wrote an article describing the new Vinex housing developments as 'suburbia for beginners' (*NRC Handelsblad*, 1 April 2000).

25   A. Hoogewoning (ed.), 'Market Supply Architecture', *Architecture in the Netherlands Yearbook 1998–1999*, Rotterdam: NAI Publishers, 1999.

26   H. Lorzing, 'Reinventing Suburbia in the Netherlands', *Built Environment*, 2006, 32: 3, p. 299.

27   A. Hoogewoning (ed.), 'Market Supply Architecture', *Architecture in the Netherlands Yearbook 1998–1999*, Rotterdam: NAI Publishers, 1999, p. 24.

28   Ibid.

29   Ibid.

30   H. Ibelings, *The Artificial Landscape: Contemporary Architecture, Urbanism, and Landscape Architecture in the Netherlands*, Rotterdam: NAI Publishers, 2000, p. 66.

31   Cited in Ministry of Housing, Spatial Planning and the Environment, *What People Want, Where People Live: Housing in the 21st Century*, The Hague: Communication Directorate, 2001.

32   Ministry of Housing, Spatial Planning and the Environment, *What People Want, Where People Live: Housing in the 21st Century*, The Hague: Communication Directorate, 2001, p. 30.

33   J. E. Abrahamse (ed.), Marlies Buurman, Bernard Hulsman, Hans Ibelings, Allard Jolles, Ed Melet and Ton Schaap, *Eastern Harbour District Amsterdam: Urbanism and Architecture*, Rotterdam: NAI Publishers, 2003, p. 204.

34   Ibid., p. 205.

35   Ibid.

36   L. Melchert, 'The Dutch Sustainable Building Policy: A Model for Developing Countries?', *Building and Environment*, 42:2, 2007, p. 895.

37   Dienst Ruimtelijke Ordening en Economische Zaken, *Zorgen Voor Morgen*, Hulpverleningsdienst, Groningen: Dienst Informatie en Administratie, 1988.

38   Cited in L. Melchert, 'The Dutch Sustainable Building Policy: A Model for Developing Countries?', *Building and Environment*, 42: 2, 2007, pp. 893–901.

39   Ibid.

40   L. Clarke and C. Wall, *Skills and the Construction Process: A Comparative Study of the Vocational Training and Quality in Social Housebuilding*, Bristol: The Policy Press, 1996, p. 3.

41   Ibid.

42   Ministry of Housing, Spatial Planning and the Environment, *What People Want, Where People Live: Housing in the 21st Century*, The Hague: Communication Directorate, 2001, p. 14.

43   Ibid., p. 20.

44   R. Rogers, *Housing for a Compact City*, London: GLA Architecture and Urbanism Unit, 2000.

45   W. Hemmingway, 'Holistic Housing', *Urban Design Quarterly* 86, 2003, 11.

46   R. Pistor (ed.), *A City in Progress: Physical Planning in Amsterdam*, Amsterdam: Ruimtelijke Ordening, 1994, p. 81.

47   E. Hoppenbrouwer and E. Louw, 'Mixed Use Development', *European Planning Studies*, 13: 7, 2005, p. 975.

48   L. Deben (ed.), W. Salet (ed.) and M. T. van Thoor, *Cultural Heritage and the Future of the Historic Inner City of Amsterdam*, Amsterdam: Aksant, 2004, p. 305.

49   Ibid.

50   Ibid.

51   E. Hoppenbrouwer and E. Louw, 'Mixed Use Development', *European Planning Studies*, 13: 7, 2005, p. 980.

52   Ibid.

53   Ibid.

54   Ibid., p. 981.

55   J. E. Abrahamse (ed.), Marlies Buurman, Bernard Hulsman, Hans Ibelings, Allard Jolles, Ed Melet and Ton Schaap, *Eastern Harbour District Amsterdam: Urbanism and Architecture*, Rotterdam: NAI Publishers, 2003, p. 124.

56   F. Claus, F. van Dongen and T. Schaap, *Ijburg, Haveneiland and Rieteilanden*, Rotterdam: 010 Publishers, 2001, p. 72.

57   Ibid.

58   SmartAgent Company, *Appendix II.4: Summary of a Consumer Satisfaction Survey for Vathorst*, SmartAgent Company, March 27, 2007.

59   Leidsche Rijn Information Centre, *Leidsche Rijn Masterplan: Summary in English*, Leidsche Rijn: Leidsche Rijn Information Centre, 2000.

Two
Design quality in the United Kingdom

1   Former Architecture and Urbanism Unit at the Greater London Authority, now Design for London, *Housing Provision: The London Plan*, London: Greater London Authority, 2004.

2   Llewelyn Davies, *Sustainable Residential Quality: Exploring the Housing Potential of Large Sites*, London: LPAC, 2000.

3   Department of the Environment, Crown Copyright, *Quality in Town and Country: Discussion Document*, 1994, London: Department of the Environment.

4   Urban Task Force, *Towards an Urban Renaissance: Final Report of the Urban Task Force*, London: Spon Press, 1999, p. 68.

5   Office of the Deputy Prime Minister, now Department for Communities and Local Government, Crown Copyright, *Sustainable Communities: Homes for All*, 2005. Online. Available HTTP: <http://www.communities.gov.uk/documents/corporate/pdf/homes-for-all> (accessed 18 December 2007).

6   Department for Communities and Local Government, Crown Copyright, *Planning Policy Statement 3: Housing, National Planning Policy*, London: DCLG Publications, 2006, p. 6.

7   Ibid.

8   Department for Communities and Local Government, Crown Copyright, *Planning Policy Statement 3: Housing, National Planning Policy*, London: DCLG Publications, 2006, p. 8.

9   Ibid.

10   Commission for Architecture and the Built Environment. Online. Available HTTP: <http://www.cabe.org.uk/default.asp> (accessed 10 December 2007).

11   Commission for Architecture and the Built Environment, *Housing Audit: Assessing the Design Quality of New Homes*, London: CABE Publications, 2004.

12   Ibid.

13   Commission for Architecture and the Built Environment, *The Housing Audit for the North East, North West and Yorkshire and Humber in the UK*, London: CABE Publications, 2005.

14   Royal Institute of British Architects, *Better Homes and Neighbourhoods, RIBA Policy Paper*, London: RIBA, 2007, p. 1.

15   Ibid., p. 3.

16   S. Prasad, *RIBA President's Inaugural Lecture,* held at the Royal Institute of British Architects, London, November 2007.

17   The Housing Corporation and Commission for Architecture and the Built Environment, *The Williams Report*, London: The Housing Corporation, 2007.

18   Department for Communities and Local Government, Crown Copyright, *Calcutt Review of Housebuilding Delivery*, London: DCLG Publications, 2007, p. 65.

19   Ibid., p. 70.

20   Department of Trade and Industry, *Lessons Learnt, Designed for Many: The Challenge to Build the £60k House*, London: English Partnerships, 2006, p. 5.

21   Former Architecture and Urbanism Unit at the Greater London Authority, now Design for London, *Recommendations for Living at Superdensity*, London: Design for Homes, 2007, p. 4.

22   M. Carmona, *Housing Design Quality, Through Policy, Guidance and Review*, London: Spon Press, 2001.

23   Former Architecture and Urbanism Unit at the Greater London Authority, now Design for London, *Recommendations for Living at Superdensity*, London, p. 4.

24   N. Gallent, and M. Tewdwr Jones, *Decent Homes for All: Planning's Evolving Role in Housing Provision*, London: Routledge, 2007.

25   Former Architecture and Urbanism Unit at the Greater London Authority, now Design for London, *Recommendations for Living at Superdensity*, London: Design for Homes, 2007; Helen Cope Consulting Ltd, Levitt Bernstein Associates and Walker Management, *Higher Density Housing for Families : A Design and Specification Guide*, London Housing Federation, London, 2004; http://www.east-thames.co.uk/highdensity/pages/overview/the_toolkit.asp.

26   Former Architecture and Urbanism Unit at the Greater London Authority, now Design for London, *Housing for a Compact City*, London, 2005, p. 19.

27   Commission for Architecture and the Built Environment, *Better Neighbourhoods: Making Higher Densities Work*, London: CABE Publications, 2004.

28   N. Gallent, and M. Tewdwr Jones, *Decent Homes for All: Planning's Evolving Role in Housing Provision*, London: Routledge, 2007.

29   Commission for Architecture and the Built Environment, *Design Coding: Testing its use in England*, London: CABE, 2005.

30   *Planning Policy Statement 3: Housing*, DCLG, 2006. Cited in: Department for Communities and Local Government, Crown Copyright, *Preparing Design Codes: A Practice Manual*, DCLG Publications, 2006, p. 13.

31   M. Carmona, S. Marshall and Q. Stevens, 'Design Codes, their Use and Potential', *Progress in Planning*, 65, 2006, p. 255.

32   Ibid.

33   Commission for Architecture and the Built Environment, *Design Coding: Testing its Use in England*, London: CABE Publications, 2005, p. 27.

34   Department for Communities and Local Government, *Preparing Design Codes: A Practice Manual*, London: DCLG Publications, 2006, p. 10.

35   M. Carmona, S. Marshall and Q. Stevens, 'Design Codes, their Use and Potential', *Progress in Planning*, 65, 2006, p. 264.

36   Ibid., p. 272.

37   Ibid.

38   Department for Communities and Local Government, *Building a Greener Future: Policy Statement*, London: DCLG Publications, 2007, p. 10.

39   Department for Communities and Local Government, *Eco-towns Prospectus*, London: DCLG Publications, 2007, p. 9.

40   Department for Communities and Local Government, *Eco-towns Prospectus,* op. cit., p. 14.

41   House of Commons, Crown Copyright, *House of Commons Environmental Audit First Report: Housing: Building a Sustainable Future*, London: The Stationery Office, 2004, p35.

42   Department of the Environment, *Quality in Town and Country: Discussion Document*, London: Department of the Environment, 1994.

43   J. Egan, *Rethinking Construction: The Report of the Construction Task Force*, London: DETR, 1998.

44   J. Egan, *The Egan Review: Skills for Sustainable Communities*, London: RIBA Enterprises, 2004.

45   Royal Institute of British Architects, *Better Homes and Neighbourhoods, RIBA Policy Paper*, London: RIBA, 2007, p. 2.

46   Commission for Architecture and the Built Environment (2003) *Building Sustainable Communities: Developing the Skills we Need*, London: CABE Publications. Online. Available HTTP: <http://www.cabe.org.uk/AssetLibrary/2253.pdf > (accessed 12 December 2007).

47   L. Revill, 'Thirteen Years On', *Urban Design Quarterly* 88, 2003, 19.

48   Mayor of London, *Housing Space Standards*, London: Greater London Authority, 2006, p. 20.

49   P. Hall, *Urban and Regional Planning*, London: Routledge, 2002, p. 33.

50   F. Jackson, *Sir Raymond Unwin: Architect, Planner and Visionary*, Architects In Perspective, London: A. Zwemmer Ltd, 1985, p. 9.

51 M. Miller, *Hampstead Garden Suburb: Arts and Crafts Utopia?*
London: Phillimore and Co., 2006, p. 54.

52 Essex County Council Planning Department, *Design Guide for
Residential Areas*, Chelmsford: Essex County Council, 1973, pp. 71–72.

53 D. Sim, *British Housing Design*, Harlow: Longman, 1993.

54 M. Miller, op. cit., p. 54.

55 I. Nairn, *Outrage*, London: Architectural Press, 1955.

56 Ministry of Housing and Local Government, Crown Copyright,
Homes for Today and Tomorrow, London: Her Majesty's Stationary
Office, 1961, p. 37.

57 V. Karn and L. Sheridan, *New Homes in the 1990s: A Study of
Design, Space and Amenity in Housing Associations and Private
Sector Production*, Manchester: Manchester University Press,
1994.

58 http://www.lifetimehomes.org.uk/pages/home.html; A. Drury,
Standards and Quality in Development: A Good Practice Guide,
London: National Housing Federation, 2008.

59 Royal Institute of British Architects, *Better Homes and
Neighbourhoods*, RIBA Policy Paper, London, 2007, p. 4.

60 Royal Institute of British Architects, *Better Homes and
Neighbourhoods*, RIBA Policy Paper, London, 2007, p. 1.

61 PRP Architects, *High Density Housing Europe: Lessons for London*,
London: East Thames Housing Group Ltd, 2002.

62 The Housing Corporation, *Design and Quality Strategy*, London:
The Housing Corporation, 2007, p. 8.

63 Department for Communities and Local Government, *Housing
Quality Indicators, Version 2*, 2005. Online. Available HTTP:
<http://www.communities.gov.uk/housing/decenthomes/
publicationsaboutdecent/housingqualityindicators> (accessed
21 January 2007).

64 Commission for Architecture and Built Environment, *Design and
Access Statements: How to Write Them and Read Them*, London:
CABE Publications, 2006. Online. Available HTTP: <http://www.
cabe.org.uk/AssetLibrary/8073.pdf> (accessed 12 December 2007).

65 M. Keith, Chair of the Thames Gateway London Partnership,
Arup, *Heroic Change, Securing Environmental Quality in Thames
Gateway, London, Introduction,* London: Thames Gateway London
Partnership, 2001.

66 J. Pickard, 'Few Takers for Green Tax Relief', *Financial Times
Weekend*, 20 January 2008.

67 Department for Communities and Local Government, Crown
Copyright, *Thames Gateway Interim Plan Policy Framework*,
London: DCLG Publications, 2006, p. 39.

68 Department for Communities and Local Government,
Crown Copyright, www.communities.gov.uk, formerly
http//www.odpm.com. Online. Available HTTP:
<http://www.odpm.com > (accessed 10 January 2006).

69 Department for Communities and Local Government, Crown
Copyright, *The Delivery Plan: The Thames Gateway,* London: DCLG
Publications, 2007, p. 8.

70 Ibid., p. 45.

71 Commission for Architecture and the Built Environment, *South
East, The Thames Gateway*, 2007. Online. Available HTTP:
<http://www.cabe.org.uk/default.aspx?contentitemid=1569>
(accessed 21 January 2007).

72 Ibid.

73 L. Hanley, *Estates: An Intimate History*, London: Granta
Publications, 2007.

74 E. Hooftman, 'Is the Thames Gateway Project a Busted Flush?'
Building Design, 30 November 2007, p. 9.

75 E. Bennett, 'Gateway Houses, "Characterless"', *Building Design*,
6 January 2006.

76 P. Hall, 'The Thames Gateway: Here be Monsters', *Guardian*,
29 October 2003.

77 R. Rogers, 'Dan Dare and Doll's Houses: Will it be the Architects
or the Vandals who build the Thames Gateway?' *Guardian*,
29 January 2005.

78 Ibid.

79 Ibid.

80 I. Abley, *The Sustainable Communities Initiative is a Further
Attack on Professionalism*, 2007. Online. Available HTTP:
<http://www.audacity.org> (accessed 15 June 2007).

81 Department for Communities and Local Government, Crown
Copyright, *Thames Gateway Interim Plan Policy Framework*,
London: DCLG Publications, 2006, p. 40.

82 Department for Communities and Local Government, Crown
Copyright, *Calcutt Review of Housebuilding Delivery,* London:
DCLG Publications, 2007, p. 63.

83 Home Builders Federation, Crown Copyright, *Calcutt Review of
Housebuilding Delivery, Submission by Home Builders Federation*,
London: HBF, 2007.

84 Department for Communities and Local Government, Crown
Copyright, *Calcutt Review of Housebuilding Delivery*, London:
DCLG Publications, 2007, p. 63.

85 Campaign to Protect Rural England, *Thames Gateway: From
Rhetoric to Reality*, London: CPRE Publications, 2005, p. 26.

86 B. Van de Burgwal, M. Van Acht, Z. Van der Veen, *De Staat van Amersfoort, MonitorLeefbaarheid en Veiligheid*, Amersfoort: Gemeente Amersfoort, 2007.

87 The meaning of social cohesion relates to a cohesive community in which inhabitants feel a shared sense of belonging and an ability to contribute to it.

88 E. Bennett, 'Gateway Houses, "Characterless"', *Building Design*, 6 January 2006.

89 Department of Environment, Transport and the Regions, Crown Copyright, *Millennium Villages and Sustainable Communities*, London: DETR, 1999, p. 7.

90 Ibid., p. 13.

91 C. Holmes, *A New Vision for Housing*, London: Routledge, 2006, p. 84.

92 A. Gilligan, *Britain's Bad Housing, Broadcast*, 7 July 2007, 8pm, Channel 4.

93 G. Towers, *An Introduction to Urban Design: At Home in the City*, Oxford: Architectural Press, 2005, p. 72.

94 J. Daly, G. Pattinger and T. Dixon, *Residential Investment and Sustainable Communities*, Reading: The College of Estate Management, 2003, p. 99.

95 Countryside Properties, Taylor Woodrow and English Partnerships, *Welcome to Greenwich Millennium Village*, 2000. Online. Available HTTP: <http://www.greenwich-village.co.uk/index_main.htm> (accessed 21 January 2007).

96 W. Hemingway, *One Staiths South Bank: A Dynamic New Concept in Housing*, Wimpey Homes Homelife, 2006.

97 Peter Barber Architects, *Donnybrook Quarter Competition Text*, 2002. Online. Available HTTP: <http://www.peterbarberarchitects.com/01_Donny.html (accessed 21 January 2007).

Three
Learning from the Netherlands: design quality in new housing in the UK and the Netherlands

1 R. Rogers, 'Dan Dare and Doll's Houses: Will it be the Architects or the Vandals who build Thames Gateway?' *Guardian*, 29 January 2005.

2 The author in conversation with Wim Van Weelan, CEO Ontwilikelings Bedieyt Vathoest, at the Vathorst Information Centre on 23 December 2007.

3 F. Claus, F. van Dongen and T. Schaap, *Ijburg, Haveneiland and Rieteilanden*, Rotterdam: 010 Publishers, 2001, p. 69.

4 E. Woodman, 'Works', *Building Design*, 5 May 2006.

5 A. De Botton, 'Repeat Business', *Building Design*, 12 May 2006.

6 H. French (ed.), *Accommodating Change*, London: Circle 33 Housing Group, 2002.

7 M. Carmona, S. Marshall and Q. Stevens, 'Design Codes, their Use and Potential', *Progress in Planning*, 65, 2006, p. 243.

8 J. Greer, 'The Route to Quality Housing, Letter of the Week', *Building Design,* 25 May 2007, p. 8.

9 Ibid.

10 Mayor of London, *Housing Space Standards*, London: Greater London Authority, 2006, p. 18.

11 Ibid., Appendix 9, p. 9.

12 Ibid., p. 18.

13 Department for Communities and Local Government, Crown Copyright, *Calcutt Review of Housebuilding Delivery*, London: DCLG Publications, 2007, p. 7.

14 Mayor of London, *Housing Space Standards*, London: Greater London Authority, 2006, p. 27.

15 V. Karn and L. Sheridan, *New Homes in the 1990s: A Study of Design, Space and Amenity in Housing Associations and Private Sector Production*, Manchester: Manchester University Press, 1994.

16 Mayor of London, *Housing Space Standards*, London: Greater London Authority, 2006, p. 18.

17 W. Hemingway, 'One Staiths South Bank: A Dynamic New Concept in Housing', *Wimpey Homes Homelife*, 2006.

18 J. E. Abrahamse (ed.), Marlies Buurman, Bernard Hulsman, Hans Ibelings, Allard Jolles, Ed Melet and Ton Schaap, *Eastern Harbour District Amsterdam: Urbanism and Architecture*, Rotterdam: NAI Publishers, 2003, p. 124.

19 W. Hemingway, 'One Staiths South Bank: A Dynamic New Concept in Housing', *Wimpey Homes Homelife*, 2006.

20 Department for Communities and Local Government, Crown Copyright, *Calcutt Review of Housebuilding Delivery*, London: DCLG Publications, 2007, p. 63.

21 B. Van de Burgwal, M. Van Acht, Z. Van der Veen, *De Staat van Amersfoort, MonitorLeefbaarheid en Veiligheid*, Amersfoort: Gemeente Amersfoort, 2007.

22 Ibid., p. 51.

23 Ibid., p. 29.

24 Ibid.

25 Department for Communities and Local Government, Crown Copyright, *Calcutt Review of Housebuilding Delivery*, London: DCLG Publications, 2007, p. 63.

26   Scottish Executive, Crown Copyright, *A Policy on Architecture For Scotland: Public Consultation Review of Policy*, Edinburgh: Scottish Executive, 2006.

27   House of Commons , ODPM Housing, Planning, Local Government and the Regions Committee, *The Role and Effectiveness of CABE: Fifth Report of the Session*, 2005, section 6, p. 31.

28   WWF-UK, *One Million Sustainable Homes Brief*, Godalming: WWF, 2004, p. 9.

29   SmartAgent Company, *Appendix II.4: Summary of a Consumer Satisfaction Survey for Vathorst*, SmartAgent Company, March 27, 2007.

30   Harlow Renaissance Ltd, *Harlow Renaissance Study Tour Report, Learning from Dutch New Towns and Suburbs*, London: URBED, 2007, pp. 10-11. Online. Available HTTP: <http://wwww.urbed.co.uk> (accessed 15 June 2007).

31   VROM, *Housing Production and Renovation*, 2007. Online. Available HTTP: <http://international.vrom.nl/pagina.html> (accessed 31 August 2007).

32   Department for Communities and Local Government, Crown Copyright, *Calcutt Review of Housebuilding Delivery*, London: DCLG Publications, 2007, p. 18.

33   B. Van de Burgwal, M. Van Acht, Z. Van der Veen, *De Staat van Amersfoort, MonitorLeefbaarheid en Veiligheid*, Amersfoort: Gemeente Amersfoort, 2007.

34   Commission for Architecture and the Built Environment, *Paving the Way: How to Achieve Clean, Safe and Attractive Streets*, London: Thomas Telford Books, 2002, p. 27.

Conclusion

1   I. Abley, *The Sustainable Communities Initiative is a Further Attack on Professionalism*, 2007. Online. Available HTTP: < http://www.audacity.org> (accessed 15 June 2007).

2   Construction Industry Council, *Design Quality Indicator Online*, 2003. Online. Available HTTP: <http://www.dqi.org.uk/DQI/Common/DQIOnline.pdf> (accessed 21 January 2007).

3   Commission for Architecture and the Built Environment, *Design Review: Frequently Asked Questions*, 2007. Online. Available HTTP: <http://www.cabe.org.uk/default.aspx?contentitemid=1681#7> (accessed 21 January 2007).

Bibliography

Abley, I., *The Sustainable Communities Initiative is a Further Attack on Professionalism*, 2007. Online. Available HTTP: < http://www.audacity.org.> (accessed 15 June 2007).

Abley, I. and Woudhuyson, J., *Why is Construction so Backward?*, London: Wiley-Academy, 2004.

Abrahamse, J. E. (ed.), Marlies Buurman, Bernard Hulsman, Hans Ibelings, Allard Jolles, Ed Melet and Ton Schaap, *Eastern Harbour District Amsterdam, Urbanism and Architecture,* Rotterdam: NAI Publishers, 2003.

Architecture Foundation, The, *New Architects 2: A Guide to Britain's Best Young Architectural Practices,* London: Merrell, 2001.

Arup, O., 'Future Problems Facing the Designer', paper presented at Royal Society Discussion Meeting on Building Technology in the 1980s, November 1971.

Arup, O., *Heroic Change: Securing Environmental Quality in Thames Gateway, London, Introduction*, London: Thames Gateway London Partnership, 2001.

Audit Commission, *Building in Quality: A Study of Developmental Control*, London: Audit Commission, 1992.

Baart, T., Metz, T. and Tjerk, R., *Atlas of Change: Rearranging the Netherlands*, Amsterdam: NAI Publishers, 2000.

Bakker, D., Jolles, A., Provoost, M. and Wagenaar, C. (eds), *Architecture in the Netherlands Yearbook, 2005–2006*, Rotterdam: NAI Uitgevers Publishers, 2005.

Bakker, D., Jolles, A., Provoost, M. and Wagenaar, C. (eds), *Architecture in the Netherlands Yearbook, 2006–2007*, Rotterdam: NAI Uitgevers Publishers, 2006.

Balchin, P. (ed.), *Housing Policy in Europe*, London: Routledge, 1996.

Baldock, H., 'Thinking Big', Building, *Building Design*, 8 September 2000.

Ball, M., *Investing in New Housing: Lessons for the Future*, Bristol: The Policy Press, 1996.

Ball, M., *A Troubled Relationship*, Bristol: The Policy Press, 1998.

Barbieri, U. and Leen Van Duin S. (eds), *A Hundred Years of Dutch Architecture 1901–2000: Trends, Highlights*, Amsterdam: SUN, 2003.

Barker Review of Housing Supply, *Delivering Stability: Securing our Future Needs*, Final Report, London, March 2004.

Barlow, J., Cohen, M., Ashok, J. and Simpson, Y., *Towards Positive Partnering: Revealing the Realities of the Construction Industry*, Bristol: The Policy Press, 1997.

Bennett, E., 'Gateway Houses, "Characterless"', *Building Design*, 6 January 2006.

Berg, J. J., Baeten, J.P. and Patteeuw, V., *Living in the Lowlands: The Dutch Domestic Scene 1850–2004*, Rotterdam: NAI Publilshers, 2004.

Betsky, A., *False Flat: Why Dutch Design is So Good*, London: Phaidon, 2004.

Birkbeck, D. and Scoones, A. (eds), *Prefabulous Homes: The New Housebuilding Agenda*, London: The Building Centre Trust, 2007.

Blijstra, R., *Dutch Architecture after 1900*, Amsterdam: P.N. van Kampen and Zoon N.V., 1966.

Boelhouwer, P., 'The Disfunctionality of the Dutch Housing Market: Exploding House Prices Versus Falling Housing Production', paper presented at the ENHR conference, Cambridge, July 2004.

Bosma, K., Van Hoogstraten, D. and Vos, M., *Housing for the Millions: John Habraken and the SAR 1960–2000,* Rotterdam: NAI Publishers, 2000.

Bramley, G., Bartlett, W. and Lambert, C., *Planning the Market and Private Housebuilding*, London: UCL Press, 1995.

Bramley, G., Munro, M. and Pawson, H., *Key Issues in Housing: Policies and Markets in 21st Century Britain*, London: Palgrave Macmillan, 2004.

Breheny, M. and Hall, P. (eds), *The People – Where Will They Go? National Report of the TCPA Regional Inquiry into Housing Need and Provision in England.* London: The Town and Country Planning Association, 2003.

Brenton, M., *We're in Charge: CoHousing Communities of Older People in the Netherlands: Lessons for Britain?* Bristol: The Policy Press, 1998.

Buch, J., *A Century of Architecture in the Netherlands, 1880/1990*, Rotterdam: NAI Publishers, 1990.

Burdett, R., 'More Vision Needed for Thames Gateway', *Building Design*, 21 January 2005.

Campaign to Protect Rural England, *Building on Barker*, London: CPRE, 2005.

Campaign to Protect Rural England, *Thames Gateway: From Rhetoric to Reality*, London: CPRE Publications, 2005.

Carmona M., Carmona, S. and Gallent, N., *Working Together: A Guide for Planners and Housing Providers*, London: Thomas Telford, 2001.

Carmona, M., *Housing Design Quality Through Policy, Guidance and Review*, London: Spon Press, 2001.

Carmona, M., Carmona, S. and Gallent, N., *Delivering New Homes: Processes, Planners and Providers*, London: Routledge, 2003.

Carmona, M., Marshall, S., and Stevens, Q., 'Design Codes: Their Use and Potential', *Progress in Planning* 65, 2006.

Carmona, M., Punter, J. and Chapman, D., *From Design Policy to Design Quality: The Treatment of Design in Community Strategies, Local Development Frameworks and Action Plans*, London: Thomas Telford, 2002.

Christiaanse, K., Ibelings, H. and van Otterloo, G., *Strip*, Rotterdam: NAI Publishers, 2003.

Clarke, L., *Building Capitalism: Historical Change and the Labour Process in the Production of the Built Environment*, London: Routledge, 1992.

Clarke, L. and Wall, C., *A Blueprint for Change: Construction Skills Training in Britain*, London: The Policy Press, 1997.

Clarke, L. and Wall, C., 'UK Construction Skills in the Context of European Developments', *Construction Management and Economics*, 1998, 15, 553–67.

Clarke, L. and Wall, C., *Skills and the Construction Process: A Comparative Study of the Vocational Training and Quality in Social Housebuilding*, Bristol: The Policy Press, 1996.

Claus, F., Van Dongen, F. and Schaap, T., *Ijburg, Haveneiland and Rieteilanden*, Rotterdam: 010 Publishers, 2001.

Coleman, A., *Utopia on Trial: Vision and Reality in Planned Housing*, London: Hilary Shipman, 1990.

Commission for Architecture and the Built Environment, *The Value of Housing Design*, London: CABE Publications, 1994.

Commission for Architecture and the Built Environment, *Creating Excellent Buildings: A Guide for Clients*, London: CABE Publications, 2003.

Commission for Architecture and the Built Environment, *Paving the Way: How to Achieve Clean, Safe and Attractive Streets*, London: Thomas Telford Books, 2002.

Commission for Architecture and the Built Environment, *Building Sustainable Communities: Developing the Skills we Need*, London: CABE Publications, 2003. Online. Available HTTP: <http://www.cabe.org.uk/AssetLibrary/2253.pdf> (accessed 12 December 2007).

Commission for Architecture and the Built Environment, *Better Neighbourhoods: Making Higher Densities Work*, London: CABE Publications, 2004.

Commission for Architecture and the Built Environment, *Housing Audit: Assessing the Design Quality of New Homes*, London: CABE Publications, 2004.

Commission for Architecture and the Built Environment, *Design Reviewed: Masterplans*, London: CABE Publications, 2004.Commission for

Architecture and the Built Environment, *Design Coding: Testing its Use in England*, London: CABE Publications, 2005.

Commission for Architecture and the Built Environment, *The Housing Audit for the North East, North West and Yorkshire and Humber in the UK*, London: CABE Publications, 2005.

Commission for Architecture and the Built Environment, *Design Coding: Testing its use in England*, London: CABE, 2005.

Commission for Architecture and the Built Environment, *Design Review: How CABE Evaluates Quality in Architecture and Urban Design*, London: CABE Publications, 2006.

Commission for Architecture and the Built Environment, *Design Review: Frequently Asked Questions*, 2007. Online. Available HTTP: <http://www.cabe.org.uk/default.aspx?contentitemid=1681#7> (accessed 21 January 2007).

Commission for Architecture and the Built Environment, *South East: The Thames Gateway*, 2007. Online. Available HTTP: <http://www.cabe.org.uk/default.aspx?contentitemid=1569> (accessed 21 January 2007).

Construction Industry Council, *Design Quality Indicator Online*, 2003. Online. Available HTTP: <http://www.dqi.org.uk/DQI/Common/DQIOnline.pdf> (accessed 21 January 2007).

Countryside Properties, Taylor Woodrow and English Partnerships, *Welcome to Greenwich Millennium Village*, 2000. Online. Available HTTP: <http://www.greenwich-village.co.uk/index_main.htm> (accessed 21 January 2007).

Crimson with Michael Speaks and Gerard Hadders, *Mart Stam's Trousers: Stories from behind the Scenes of Dutch Moral Modernism*, Rotterdam: 010 Publishers, 1999.

Daly, J., Pattinger G., and Dixon, T., *Residential Investment and Sustainable Communities*, Reading: The College of Estate Management, 2003.

De Botton, A., 'Repeat Business', *Building Design*, 12 May 2006.

Deben, L., (ed.), Salet, W. (ed.) and Van Thoor, M. T., *Cultural Heritage and the Future of the Historic Inner City of Amsterdam*, Amsterdam: Aksant, 2004.

Department for Communities and Local Government, Crown Copyright, *Housing Quality Indicators, Version 2*, 2005. Online. Available HTTP: <http://www.communities.gov.uk/housing/decenthomes/publicationsaboutdecent/housingqualityindicators> (accessed 21 January 2007).

Department for Communities and Local Government, Crown Copyright, *Planning Policy Statement 3: Housing, National Planning Policy*, London: DCLG Publications, 2006.

Department for Communities and Local Government, Crown Copyright, *Preparing Design Codes: A Practice Manual*, London: DCLG Publications, 2006.

Department for Communities and Local Government, Crown Copyright, *Thames Gateway Interim Plan Policy Framework*, London: DCLG Publications, 2006.

Department for Communities and Local Government, Crown Copyright, www.communities.gov.uk, formerly http//www.odpm.com. Available HTTP: <http://www.odpm.com> (accessed 10 January 2006).Department for Communities and Local Government, Crown Copyright, *Calcutt Review of Housebuilding Delivery*, London: DCLG Publications, 2007.

Department for Communities and Local Government, Crown Copyright, *Building a Greener Future, Policy Statement,* London: DCLG Publications, 2007.

Department for Communities and Local Government, Crown Copyright, *Eco-towns Prospectus*, London: DCLG Publications, 2007.

Department for Communities and Local Government, Crown Copyright, *The Delivery Plan: The Thames Gateway*, London: DCLG Publications, 2007.

Department for Transport, Local Government and the Regions/CABE, *By Design: Better Places to Live: A Companion Guide to PPG3*, Tonbridge: Thomas Telford, 2001.

Department of Environment, Transport and the Regions, Crown Copyright, *Millennium Villages and Sustainable Communities*, London: DETR, 1999.

Department of Environment, Transport and the Regions, Crown Copyright, *Our Towns and Cities: The Future: Delivering an Urban Renaissance*, London: DETR, 2000.

Department of Environment, Transport and the Regions, Crown Copyright, *Quality and Choice: A Decent Home for All: The Housing Green Paper*, London: DETR, 2000.

Department of Environment, Transport and the Regions, Crown Copyright, *Regional Planning Guidance for the South East (RPG 9)*, London: DETR, 2001.

Department of Environment, Transport and the Regions, Crown Copyright, *Thames Gateway Review: Final Report*, London: DETR, 2001.

Department of the Environment, Crown Copyright, *Quality in Town and Country: Discussion Document*, 1994, London: Department of the Environment.

Department of Trade and Industry, Crown Copyright, *Lessons Learnt, Designed for Many: The Challenge to Build the £60k House*, London: English Partnerships, 2006.

Deputy Prime Minister's Construction Task Force, 1998, cited in D. Gann, *Flexibility and Choice in Housing,* Bristol: The Policy Press, 1999.

Dienst Ruimtelijke Ordening en Economische Zaken, *Zorgen Voor Morgen*, Hulpverleningsdienst, Groningen: Dienst Informatie en Administratie, 1988.

Dutt, A. and Costa, F. (eds), *Public Planning in the Netherlands: Perspectives and Change since the Second World War*, Oxford: Oxford University Press, 1985.

Education, Culture and Science, Housing, Spatial Planning and the Environment, Transport, Public Works and Water Management, Agriculture, Nature Management and Fisheries, *Architectural Policy 2001–2004: The Architecture of Space: Shaping the Netherlands*, The Hague: Education, Culture and Science, Housing, Spatial Planning and the Environment, Transport, Public Works and Water Management, Agriculture, Nature Management and Fisheries, 1996.

Egan, J., *Rethinking Construction: The Report of the Construction Task Force*, London: DETR, 1998.

Egan, J., *The Egan Review: Skills for Sustainable Communities*, London: RIBA Enterprises, 2004.

English Partnerships, *Millennium Communities: Tomorrow's Homes Today*, London: English Partnerships, 2005.

Essex County Council Planning Department, *Design Guide for Residential Areas*, Chelmsford: Essex County Council, 1973.

Faludi, A. and Van der Valk, A., *Rule and Order: Dutch Planning Doctrine in the Twentieth Century*, Dordrecht: Kluwer Academic Publishers, 1994.

Former Architecture and Urbanism Unit at the Greater London Authority, now Design for London, *Housing Provision: The London Plan*, London: Greater London Authority, 2004.

Former Architecture and Urbanism Unit at the Greater London Authority, now Design for London, *Housing for a Compact City*, London: Greater London Authority, 2005.

Former Architecture and Urbanism Unit at the Greater London Authority, now Design for London, *Recommendations for Living at Superdensity*, London: Design for Homes, 2007.

Gallent, N. and Tewdwr Jones, M., *Decent Homes for All: Planning's Evolving Role in Housing Provision*, London: Routledge, 2007.

Gann, D., *Flexibility and Choice in Housing*, Bristol: The Policy Press, 1999.

Gann, D. and Salter, A., *Interdisciplinary Skills for Built Environment Professionals: A Scoping Study*, London: The Ove Arup Foundation, 1999.

Gilligan, A., *Britain's Bad Housing, Broadcast*, 7 July 2007, 8pm, Channel 4.

Glancey, J., 'The Thames Gateway: Here be Monsters', *Guardian*, 29 October 2003.

Gray, C., *Value for Money: Helping the UK Afford the Buildings it Likes*, Reading: Reading Construction Forum, 1996.

Greater London Authority, *Accessible London: Achieving an Inclusive Environment: Lifetime Homes*, London: Greater London Authority, 2006.

Greer, J., 'The Route to Quality Housing, Letter of the Week', *Building Design*, 25 May 2007.

Grinberg, D., *Housing in the Netherlands 1900–1940*, Rotterdam: Delft University Press, 1977.

Groenendijk, P. and Vollaard, P., *Guide to Modern Architecture in Rotterdam*, Rotterdam: 010 Publishers, 1996.

Hall, P., *Urban and Regional Planning*, London: Routledge, 2002.

Hanley, L., *Estates: An Intimate History*, London: Granta Publications, 2007.

Harlow Renaissance Ltd, *Harlow Renaissance Study Tour Report: Learning from Dutch New Towns and Suburbs*, London: URBED, 2007, pp. 10-11. Online. Available HTTP: <http://wwww.urbed.co.uk> (accessed 15 June 2007).

Heathcote, E., 'What's So Good About British Architecture', *Financial Times*, 1 September 2007.

Helen Cope Consulting Ltd, Levitt Bernstein Associates and Walker Management, *Higher Density Housing for Families : A Design and Specification Guide*, London Housing Federation, London, 2004.

Hemingway, W., 'One Staiths South Bank: A Dynamic New Concept in Housing', *Wimpey Homes Homelife*, Middlesborough, 2006.

Hemmingway, W., 'Time for the Ultimate Home Makeover', *Society Guardian*, 14 June, 2002.

Hemmingway, W., 'Holistic Housing', *Urban Design Quarterly*, 86, 2003.

Holmes, C., *A New Vision for Housing*, London: Routledge, 2006.

Home Builders Federation, Crown Copyright, *Calcutt Review of Housebuilding Delivery: Submission by Home Builders Federation*, London: HBF, 2007.

Hoogewoning, A. (ed.), 'Market Supply Architecture', *Architecture in the Netherlands Yearbook 1998–1999*, Rotterdam: NAI Publishers, 1999.

Hoogewoning, A. (ed.), *Architecture in the Netherlands Yearbook, 2002–2003*, Rotterdam: NAI Uitgevers Publishers, 2002.

Hooimeijer, F. (ed.), *The Water Project: A Nineteenth-century Walk through Rotterdam*, Rotterdam: 010 Publishers, 2001.

Hoppenbrouwer, E., and Louw, E., 'Mixed Use Development', *European Planning Studies*, 13: 7, 2005.

House of Commons, Crown Copyright, *House of Commons Environmental Audit First Report: Housing: Building a Sustainable Future*, London: The Stationery Office, 2004.

House of Commons, ODPM Housing, Planning, Local Government and the Regions Committee, *The Role and Effectiveness of CABE, Fifth Report of the Session*, London: The Stationery Office Ltd, 2005.

Housing Corporation and Commission for Architecture and the Built Environment, *The Williams Report*, London: Housing Corporation, 2007.

Housing Corporation, *Design and Quality Strategy*, London: Housing Corporation, 2007.

Housing, Spatial Planning and the Environment, *Designing in the Netherlands*, The Hague: Housing, Spatial Planning and the Environment, Communication Directorate, 2000.

Hutchinson, K. and Putt, T., 'The Use of Design/Build Procurement Methods by Housing Associations', Paper held at Royal Institution of Chartered Suveyors, London, October 1992.

Ibelings, H., *Americanism, Dutch Architecture and the Transatlantic Model*, Amsterdam: NAI Publishers, 1996.

Ibelings, H., *20th Century Architecture in the Netherlands*, Rotterdam: Netherlands Architecture Institute, 1999.

Ibelings, H., *The Artificial Landscape: Contemporary Architecture, Urbanism, and Landscape Architecture in the Netherlands*, Rotterdam: NAI Publishers, 2000.

Ibelings, H., *Unmodern Architecture: Contemporary Traditionalism in the Netherlands*, Rotterdam: NAI Publishers, 2004.

Imrie, R., *Accessible Housing: Quality, Disability and Design*, London: Routledge, 2006.

International Building Exhibition Rotterdam – Hoogvliet, *WIMBY! Welcome into my Backyard!* NAI Publishers: Rotterdam, 2000.

Jackson, F., *Sir Raymond Unwin: Architect, Planner and Visionary*, Architects In Perspective, London: A. Zwemmer Ltd, 1985.

Karn, V. and Sheridan, L., *New Homes in the 1990s*, Manchester: Manchester University Press, 1994.

Keith, M., Chair of the Thames Gateway London Partnership, Arup, *Heroic Change: Securing Environmental Quality in Thames Gateway, London: Introduction*, London: Thames Gateway London Partnership, 2001.

Kendall, S. and Teicher, J., *Residential Open Buildings*, London: E and FN Spon, 2000.

Kloos, M. (Ed), *Amsterdam in Detail*, Rotterdam: Arcam, 1996.

Koos, M. and Wendt, D., *Formats for Living: Contemporary Floor Plans in Amsterdam,* Amsterdam: Architectur and Natura Press, 2000.

Koster, E. and Van Oeffelt, T., *Hoogbouw in Netherland 1990–2000: High Rise in the Netherlands,* Rotterdam: NAI Publishers, 1997.

Latham, M, *Constructing the Team: Final Report of the Government/Industry Review of Procurement and Contractual Arrangements in the Construction Industry,* London: HMSO, 1996.

Lazell, M., 'UK's Lack of Planning Vision "Tragic" says Farrell', *Building Design,* 14 September 2007.

Leishman, C., Aspinall, P., Munro, M. and Warren, F., *Preferences, Quality and Choice in New-Build Housing,* York: Joseph Rowntree Foundation, 2004.

Lewis, S., *Front to Back: A Design Agenda for Urban Housing,* London: Architectural Press, 2005.

Llewelyn Davies, *Sustainable Residential Quality\; Exploring the Housing Potential of Large Sites,* London: LPAC, 2000.

Llewelyn Davies, *Urban Design Compendium,* London: Llewelyn Davies, 2000.

London Thames Gateway, *Development and Investment Framework,* London: Greater London Authority, 2004.

Lootsma, B., *SuperDutch, New Architecture in the Netherlands,* London: Thames and Hudson, 2000.

Lorzing, H., 'Reinventing Suburbia in the Netherlands', *Built Environment,* 2006, 32: 3.

Lund, B., *Understanding Housing Policy,* Bristol: The Policy Press, 2006.

Macmillan, S. (ed.), *Designing Better Buildings: Quality and Value in the Built Environment,* London: Spon Press, 2003.

Mayor of London, *Housing Space Standards,* London: Greater London Authority, 2006.

Melchert, L., 'The Dutch Sustainable Building Policy: A Model for Developing Countries?', *Building and Environment,* 42: 2, 2007.

Melet, E., *The Architectural Detail: Dutch Architects Visualise their Concepts,* Rotterdam: NAI Publishers, 2002.

Melis, L. (ed.), *Parasite Paradise: A Manifesto for Temporary Architecture and Flexible Urbanism,* Rotterdam: NAI Publishers, 2003.

Meusen, H. and Van Kempen, R., *Working Paper, 121: Dutch Social Rented Housing: A British Experience?* Bristol: SAUS Publications, 1994.

Miller, M., *Hampstead Garden Suburb: Arts and Crafts Utopia?* London: Phillimore and Co, 2006.

Ministry of Education, *Seminar Report: Discussing Architectural Quality: European Forum for Architectural Policies,* Helsinki: Publications of the Ministry of Education, 2003.

Ministry of Housing and Local Government, Crown Copyright, *Homes for Today and Tomorrow,* London: Her Majesty's Stationary Office, 1961.

Ministry of Housing and Physical Planning, *The Future of Old Housing Stock in the Netherlands,* The Hague: Information Service for The Hague, 1970.

Ministry of Housing and Physical Planning, *The Netherlands: Current Trends and Policies in Housing and Building in 1975,* The Hague: Information Service for The Hague, 1976.

Ministry of Housing, Spatial Planning and the Environment Communication Directorate, *Making Space, Sharing Space: Fifth National Policy Document on Spatial Planning 2000/2020,* The Hague: Communication Directorate, 2001.

Ministry of Housing, Spatial Planning and the Environment, *What People Want, Where People Live: Housing in the 21st Century,* The Hague: Communication Directorate2001.

Muir, H., and Hurst, W., 'Charles Touts Dutch Methods', *Guardian,* 22 July 2005.

MVRDV, *Farmax: Excursions on Density,* Rotterdam: 010 Publishers, 1998.

Nairn, I., *Outrage,* 1959, London: Architectural Press.

National Architecture Institute, *Fresh Facts: The Best Buildings by Young Architects in the Netherlands,* Rotterdam: NAI Publishers, 2003.

National Architecture Institute, *Living in the Lowlands: The Dutch Domestic Scene, 1850–2004,* Rotterdam: NAI Publishers, 2004.

Neal, P. (ed.), *Urban Villages and the Making of Communities,* London: Spon Press, 2003.

Needham, D., Krujit, B. and Koenders, P., *Urban Land and Property Markets in the Netherlands,* London: UCL Press, 1993.

Netherlands Institute for Spatial Research, *New Housing and Mobility: An Analysis of the Vinex Spatial Mobility Policy: Summary,* Rotterdam/Den Haag: NAI Publishers, 2006. Online. Available HTTP: <http://www.rpb.nl/en-gb/> (accessed on 13 December 2007).

Netherlands Institute for Spatial Research, *Vinex: A Morphological Exploration,* Rotterdam/Den Haag: NAI Publishers, 2006. Online. Available HTTP: <http://www.rpb.nl/en-gb/> (accessed on 13 December 2007).

Office of the Deputy Prime Minister, now Department for Communities and Local Government, Crown Copyright, *Delivering Planning Policy for Housing: PPG3 Implementation Study,* London: ODPM, 2003.

Office of the Deputy Prime Minister, now Department for Communities and Local Government, Crown Copyright, *Evaluating the Impact of Design Awards for Housing,* London: RIBA Enterprises, 2004.

Office of the Deputy Prime Minister, now Department for Communities and Local Government, Crown Copyright, *Sustainable Communities: Homes for All*, 2005. Online. Available HTTP: <http://www.communities.gov.uk/documents/corporate/pdf/homes-for-all> (accessed 18 December 2007).

Ostojski, P. (ed.), *Kop Van Zuid*, Rotterdam: 010 Publishers, 1999.

Pawley, M., *Architecture Versus Housing*, London: Studio Vista, 1971.

Peter Barber Architects, *Donnybrook Quarter Competition Text*, 2002. Online. Available HTTP: <http://www.peterbarberarchitects.com/01_Donny.html (accessed 21 January 2007).

Pickard, J., 'Few Takers for Green Tax Relief', *Financial Times Weekend*, 20 January 2008.

Pistor, R. (ed.), *A City in Progres: Physical Planning in Amsterdam*, Amsterdam: Ruimtelijke Ordening, 1994.

Prasad, S., 'Measuring Quality and Value: Inclusive Maps', in S. Macmillan, *Designing Better Buildings, Quality and Value in the Built Environment,* London: Spon Press, 2003.

Prasad, S., *RIBA President's Inaugural Lecture*, held at the Royal Institute of British Architects, London, November 2007.

Prix de Rome, *Urban Design, Landscape and Architecture*, Rotterdam: 010 Publishers, 2001.

Provoost, M., *Dutchtown: A City Center, Design by OMA/ Rem Koolhaas*, Rotterdam: NAI Publishers, 1998.

PRP Architects, *High Density Housing Europe: Lessons for London*, London: East Thames Housing Group Ltd, 2002.

Ravesteyn, N. Van and Evers, D., *Unseen Europe: A Survey of EU Politics and its Impact on Spatial Development in the Netherlands*, Rotterdam: NAI Publishers, 2004.

Revill, L., 'Thirteen Years On', *Urban Design Quarterly*, 88, 2003.

Rogers, R., 'Dan Dare and Doll's Houses: Will it be the Architects or the Vandals who Build the Thames Gateway?', *Guardian*, 29 January 2005.

Rogers, R., *Housing for a Compact City*, London: GLA Architecture and Urbanism Unit, 2000.

Rogers, R. and Fisher, M., *A New London*, London: Penguin, 1992.

Royal Institute of British Architects, *Better Homes and Neighbourhoods: RIBA Policy Paper*, London: RIBA, 2007.

Saunders, W., *Judging Architectural Value*, Minneapolis, MN: University of Minnesota Press, 2007.

Shetter, Z., *The Netherlands in Perspective: The Organisations of Society and Environment*, Leiden: Uitgeverij Martinus Nijhoff, 1987.

TNO BOUW, *High-rise Housing in the Netherlands: Past, Present and Sustainability Outlook*, The Hague: Ministry for Spatial Planning and Environment, 2004.

Towers, G., *An Introduction to Urban Design: At Home in the City*, Oxford: Architectural Press, 2005.

Urban Task Force, *Towards an Urban Renaissance: Final Report of the Urban Task Force*, London: Spon Press, 1999.

Van Blerk, H. and Dettmar, J., *9 + 1 Young Dutch Landscape Architects*, Rotterdam: NAI Publishers, 1999.

Van Dijk, H., 'Anarchical Housing Consumers', *Architecture in the Netherlands Yearbook 1998–1999,* Rotterdam: NAI Publishers, 1999.

Vletter, M. de, *The Critical Seventies: Architecture and Urban Planning in the Netherlands, 1968–1982*, Rotterdam: NAI Publishers, 2005.

VROM, *General Data*, 2007. Online. Available HTTP: <http://international.vrom.nl/pagina.html> (accessed 31 August 2007).

VROM, *Housing Production and Renovation*, 2007. Online. Available HTTP: <http://international.vrom.nl/pagina.html> (accessed 31 August 2007).

VROM, *Housing, Spatial Planning and the Environment*, 2007. Online. Available HTTP: <http://www.sharedspaces.nl/pagina.html?id=7328> (accessed 31 August 2007).

Vroom, M.J. and Meeus, J.H.A. (eds), *Learning from Rotterdam: Investigating the Process of Urban Park Design*, London: Mansell, 1990.

Vuijste, H., and Hooker, M.T., *The Politically Correct Netherlands since the 1960s*, Westport, CT: Greenwood Press, 2000.

Woodman, E., 'Works', *Building Design*, 5 May 2006.

WWF-UK, *One Million Sustainable Homes: Brief*, Godalming: WWF, 2004.

Zaero-Polo, A., 'A Scientific Autobiography', *Harvard Design Magazine*, fall 2004/winter 2005.

Index

Page numbers in italic denote an illustration

Image credits

The author and publisher would like to thank the following individuals
and institutions for giving permission to reproduce illustrations.
We have made every effort to contact copyright holders, but if any errors
have been made we would be happy to correct them at a later printing.

All photographs are the author's own unless otherwise stated.
All numbers refer to pages.

Alison Brooks Architects: 71, 98 (bottom)

Baan, Iwan: 14, 23, 50, 53 (top)

Bolhuis, Peter van / PANDION: ii

BoLok House: 76 (top), 76 (bottom)

Churchill, David: 2

Claus en Kaan Architecten: 33 (top), 36, 37, 38

Crocker, Tim/designforhomes: 82, 96, 99, 100–101, 112, 114–116,
117 (top), 140

Crocker, Tim: 3, 93, 104, 105, 107 (bottom), 108 (top), 109, 120, 122 (top),
123–125, 131, 136

DRO Vrom / Hans Brons: 10 (top), 11 (top), 33 (bottom)

English Partnerships: 73, 106 (top)

Feilden Clegg Bradley Studios: 94 (top), 94 (bottom), 97,
98 (top and middle)

Gameren, Dick van: 61, 62

Geurst and Schulze Architecten: 14, 15 (bottom), 17 (top), 18, 54 (bottom)

Hemingway Design: 113

Hufton+Crow: front cover, 83 (top left), 83 (bottom left), 83 (right), 130

Ijburg Information Centre: 10 (top), 35

Lavington, Maccreanor: 51, 55, 64 (top), 141

Nieuw Nederland Architecten: 39

Palmboom & Van den Bout: 29, 59, 60 (top left; bottom), 133

Peter Barber Architects: 121, 122 (bottom)

Peter White / BRE: 77 (top), 77 (bottom),

Pieter Kers: 53 (bottom)

Projectbureauijburg: 35

PRP Architects: 74 (top left), 74 (bottom left), 89

Richters, Christian: 24, 63 (top), 63 (bottom)

Rogers Stirk Harbour Architects: 74 (right), 75 (bottom), 75 (top right), 80

RuralZED.com: 84 (bottom left), 84 (right)

Search Architects: 52 (top)

Shadwick, Weeber: 75 (top left)

Sheppard Robson: 84 (top left)

Smart Agent Company: 138

Telford Homes: 79

VSVV Architects: 32

West 8 Urban Design and Landscape Architecture: 4, 20,
25 (top and bottom), 26, 27 (top left), 42, 43, 44, 60 (top right),
64 (bottom), 65